Destiny Ours

Destiny Ours

"If they tell you I'm missing. . ."

Enjoy this remarkable story of how the men of the B-24 "Postville Express" and my parents, Bill & Peggy, endured and triumphed during World War II. "Let us never forget." All the best - Bill

William F. Duffy, Jr.

William F Duffey Jr.

Oct 18, 2009

Farrell Publishing
Marion, Iowa

ISBN 0-9706539-0-5
LCCN: 2001119731

Printed by: Thomson-Shore – Dexter, Michigan
Book layout & jacket design: Farrell Publishing
Technical & graphic assistance: John Foster

www.farrellpublishing.com

Janice Marie…You made this possible. Your love and support bind the pages of Destiny Ours and ensures this story will live on for generations to come.
Thank you, Bernie. I love you!
And Bill & Peggy, my parents, whose faith, love, and devotion brought life to twelve children—eight girls and four boys. This is their story.

"Peggy, if they tell you I'm missing or dead
don't believe it, I'm coming back."

Acknowledgments

In my life I've crossed and shared many paths with others. During my journey in writing Dad's story, and fulfilling his dream, many people played a role in making Destiny Ours a reality. I mentioned Jan, my wife, but there are others to whom I'm indebted, and to them I say, "Thank you for your kindness and helping me on my journey."

Gene & Anne Parker's generosity took Jan and I across the world to Malaysia where we spent six weeks retracing Dad's footsteps in researching his story. We located the crash site of the B-29 *Postville Express*, gathered scraps of the wreckage, and visited with Malays who were present that fateful morning in 1945. Gene & Anne's kindness helped provide the answers to the countless questions encountered along the way.

Jim Ellickson-Brown—Cultural Affairs Officer, American Embassy at Kuala Lumpur, Malaysia—

organized meetings with Chinese and Malays, and on each occasion transported and translated for us, simply for the love of the story we were seeking. He is a kind and generous man and his passion for history took us on exciting roads of discovery.

Dr. Zoraini Wati Abas, professor at the University of Malaya, and Major General Dato Muslim Ayob (Retired) located people in their country we could interview and launched us on our path to fill in the blanks while in Malaysia. Their guidance insured our success.

Samsudin Bin Sidek, present January 11, 1945, aided & guided American Airmen of the B-29 Superfortress away from the wreckage and into jungle hiding despite facing the Japanese enemy's penalty of death. He led us to wreckage of the big bomber and shared his stories of long ago.

Jill Krapfl for performing the enormous task of transferring to disc, three books of faded pencil and smearing ink entries that make up Dad's 1945 diary. Jill's labor was demanding and spanned several weeks, but insured these moments of history can be shared with future generations.

My *Gathering of Writers* group for their guidance, support, and critique of my work. They gave me strength and determination to see this through. Especially Clarice Flagel and Beverly Gales who brought us together and keep us coming back.

My editing and proofreading friends: Elinor Day and Martha Hanley. Elinor makes me look good. Her remarkable eye for proper usage, sentence structure, and detail helped develop a stronger story. Martha Hanley took Elinor's preparation for publication a step further by proofreading and bestowing a sort of final blessing before the manuscript reached the printer. Martha's command of the written word helped strengthen, tune, and establish the final version. I have a deep respect and admiration for these two fine women. I am forever grateful for their kindness, generosity, and love for this story.

Kay Harkness, for the times she's come to my aid and assisted in my most pressing necessity. Her objectivity and subjectivity have steered me clear of my own confusion and led me on a path to completion.

My eleven sisters & brothers for their love and support during this difficult undertaking. This is their book as much as mine. Our family will now truly grasp what our Father, as countless other fathers endured to survive and return home to loved ones after World War II.

And finally my Mother, Peggy, for her deep faith in God, powerful love for us children, and commitment to teach us the same. Throughout the writing of Destiny Ours she helped with the many questions only she could provide answers to. I am utterly amazed by this story she and my Father shared long ago. It's one story representing the countless that make up what has been coined, "The Greatest Generation."

Table of Contents

Acknowledgments 7

Introduction 15

Veterans Hospital 19

The Mission 25

Talib 59

Jungle Fever 115

Chee-Fa-Pu 125

Su-Ling-Pu 153

Two-Hundred-Mile Trek 175

Sixth Regiment Headquarters 187

British Second Detachment 213

J. Jack Bussey 233

Bussey's Camp 247

The Jap Detective 261

Japan Surrenders 271

Journey Home 303

Epilogue 311

Bill Duffy & Peggy McCormick's
Wedding Day - August 22, 1942

"DESTINY OURS"

My love for you is lasting and true,
I whisper sweet nothings at all;
Then you say to me, you'll share your love for me,
as we linger in your front hall.
Thru worry, and strife we'll cut our way like a knife,
until success and happiness is ours;
Then down the road of life we will travel as man and
wife, until we meet those immortal bars.
Then our love will be complete,
as it will be beyond defeat,
resting in the loving arms of Our Lord.

- William F. Duffy -
1938
Written to high school sweetheart:
Peggy McCormick Duffy

Capt. William F. Duffy

<u>Medals of Honor:</u>

Distinguished Flying Cross
Silver Star
Purple Heart with Oak Leaf Cluster
Air Medal with Oak Leaf Cluster
Presidential Unit Citation
Philippine Liberation Medal
Five Battle Stars Asiatic-Pacific Theatre
Asiatic-Pacific Campaign Medal
American Campaign Medal
Victory Medal WWII

Introduction

My father is only one man and one story, among countless. He doesn't show up in history books. His name is unknown except to family and friends. In the years to come his name will seldom be spoken. His time is the past; we live in the present and look toward the future. Without the past I have no future. So I write what I've come to learn about a man who walks no more, whose time fades with other unknowns.

Over the years, my knowledge of World War II has led me to appreciate the individual men and women who fought and died that we may be free of the likes of Adolph Hitler, Benito Mussolini and Emperor Hirohito. It's astonishing that they would give their lives that we may enjoy ours.

Visiting with veterans arouses empathy and a mysterious connection with all I come to know.

Each person of this war has memories, stories and experiences to share. Common knowledge are the well-known battles, the key players, the big picture—but I cherish the tale of the individual. My empathy and sentiment grow as these men approach the close of their lives. Once they leave our world, their stories and existence will fade and be forgotten, unless we keep the stories alive.

Let us never forget.

The desire to present this book is a tribute to my father. Like many during World War II, my mother and father had one child, with another on the way, when orders took Dad into combat overseas. After the war, with Dad and Mom reunited, they gave birth to ten more children. I am one of the ten.

I recall words Dad spoke near the close of his life: *"Bill, I want that book so bad!"* I grew up with his story. At times I feel I made the journey. I have based my writing on his daily diary, newspaper and magazine accounts, letters, scrapbooks, library texts, military records and interviews. I have traveled to Malaysia, where I located wreckage from his airplane and retraced his footsteps taken over fifty-five years ago. I have spent thousands of hours in research, writing and review. My efforts, though difficult and challenging, have rewarded me with this book.

My father's last breath came late in the morning of October 18, 1991. In the eight years prior, he suffered from swelling and inflammation of the joints, due to rheumatoid arthritis. Alzheimer's disease robbed him of his ability to communicate and remember people, places and events. In the final hour, at 71, it was complications of respiratory disease that took his life.

Capt. William F. Duffy

Army Air Corps B-29 Bombardier/Navigator
China-Burma-India Theatre of WWII
20th Air Force—HQ Kharagpur, India
58th Bombardment Wing, 468th Bomb Group,
793rd Squadron, *Squadron leader.*
Military flying hours: 700(combat hours: 135)

Thirty-three Missions:

Twenty-two Hump(Himalaya) missions:
Kharagpur, India to forward bases in China
transporting troops, bombs, gasoline, aircraft
parts, supplies, etc.

Twelve combat missions:
Bangkok, Siam(Thailand)----------------June 5, 1944
Yawata, Japan*--------------------------June 15, 1944
Yawata, Japan-------------------------August 20, 1944
Anshan, Manchuria----------------September 8, 1944
Okayama, Formosa(Taiwan)-------October 16, 1944
Rangoon, Burma-------------------November 3, 1944
Omura, Japan----------------------November 11, 1944
Bangkok, Siam(Thailand)--------November 27, 1944
Hankow, China--------------------December 18, 1944
Omura, Japan---------------------December 19, 1944
Cheng-Hsien, China**-----------December 21, 1944
Singapore(missing in action)-------January 11, 1945

*This mission gave Duffy the recognition of being the first
  man to drop bombs on Japan during WWII from a B-29.
**Alternate target. *Postville Express* was unable to make the
  primary target at Mukden, Manchuria.

Veterans Hospital

"I'm here to see my father, William Duffy."

Two nurses behind the station desk, both large and out of shape, glanced up. The smaller responded, "He's down the hall to the left, watching television. He's waiting for your mother." She chewed gum, the other rested her head on her hand and elbow. Their hair needed care, their white uniforms bleach. Enthusiasm would be good, and the snack food competing with paperwork on the desk seemed out of place. I wondered about their care of the patients. I turned and headed down the hall.

Passing rooms on either side, I fixed my eyes ahead, sensitive to what lay beyond each door. On the left, the hallway opened into a lounge with couch, chairs and a television mounted near the ceiling, broadcasting Sunday football. Below the television in a wheelchair was my father, his back to me, his head tilted toward the floor. No other people occupied the lounge or hallway. I paused, took a deep breath and readied my face with a smile. Facing him, I crouched down, grasped his right hand and gently squeezed, as I said, "Hi Dad, how are you doing?"

Our eyes met, and he displayed a hint of a smile. I wrapped my arms around him, pulling us close, as my face brushed against his unshaven cheek. I pressed my lips to his cheek and kissed him.

"It's nice to see you, Dad." He didn't answer; instead, he began to rise from the chair. It appeared there wasn't enough strength in him, because he managed to rise only a few inches. He pulled at the cotton robe and gown covering his chest. He tried to explain his actions, but I couldn't make any sense of the words.

I thought he needed my assistance to stand from the chair, so I grabbed his arm with both hands. As I attempted to lift, he continued the tugging at the garments covering his chest.

I couldn't lift him from the wheelchair—something held him. Upon inspection, I learned he was tied down at both sides of the chair by a restraining jacket. I felt bad about trying to force him out of the chair. I untied the straps and helped him to his feet.

He immediately headed up the hallway.

"Dad, where are you going?" I grabbed his forearm to stop his flight. I moved in front of him and grasped both arms to stop him.

"Where are you going?"

"Where's Mother?" he asked.

"She's at home, Dad."

"How come she isn't here?"

"She's coming to visit later," I lied.

Again, he attempted to head up the hall, as I fought to hold him back.

"Dad, where are you going?"

"Leave me alone," he shouted, grabbing a fistful of my sweater in each of his disfigured hands. The knuckle of each finger was inflamed and swollen from the rheumatoid arthritis that had made its home in every joint of his body for the past eight years.

The visit was tearing my heart. I had to be there, if only to satisfy the guilt and sadness I fought within. Utterly amazing, how I could accept responsibility for this disease and his being in the Veterans Hospital.

"There's Mother," Dad said, peering toward two people at the far end of the hall.

"No Dad, Mom's at home," I replied, and pulled him back toward the lounge area.

Across the back of his robe was a long strip of white tape bearing the marking, "DUFFY ROOM 424." His ID when discovered wandering the floor.

His room was across the hall from the lounge. Another piece of tape, stuck to the wall outside the door, said, "William Duffy." This was Dad's map back to his room.

I forced him into his room. He still believed Mom was down the hall.

"Let me go, you son-of-a-bitch," he fired at me.

The fierce look in his eyes and the elbow to my chest was plenty notice he was determined to be free. I had had too much experience with the temperament the Alzheimer's disease subjected its victim to and reminded myself: "It's not Dad's choice to behave in this manner." It would be anger one moment, joy the next, tears and fear would follow. Still it gnawed at my heart and hurt me to see him this way.

He walked to the bed, stopped and stared out the window. The trees still held a few leaves and the sky was cold gray. It could rain, yet the cold made me think snow. Not a pretty picture to go with this painful standoff.

He placed his hands in the pockets of the hospital robe. Here stood the man who had taught me what he knew of life. Now we couldn't even share a conversation.

Dad took a seat at the edge of his bed. I sat beside him and held his hand in mine. My eyes fell on the back of his robe, where the tape said, "DUFFY." It brought to mind a time long ago, when his name was displayed on all his clothes and gear. It was during World War II, after he had enlisted in what was then the Army Air Corps. Over the years I asked Dad to tell his story again and again. As a young boy, I never tired of Dad's memory of days past when he was a first lieutenant, then captain. Now, I'm a grown man and the story is more astounding than ever.

How I love his story. . . .

Captain William F. Duffy
XX Bomb Command HQ–468th Bomb Group
Kharagpur, India–October 2, 1944

The Mission

"Bombardier to Navigator."

"Go ahead Bombardier."

"Carl, I have sight of Tenggol Island at one o'clock." I was looking through the Plexiglas bubble, resembling a greenhouse, that makes up the nose of our B-29 bomber. My gaze locked on the green patch of land surrounded by bleached sand, plunked in the South China Sea. It was beautiful, the sea and this dab of vegetation reaching toward the morning sky, enclosed in a mist that lifted slowly with the heat of the rising sun.

The scene didn't portray our mission: "Destroy the King George VI floating dry dock at the Singapore Naval Base, in the Strait of Johore, used for repairing ships of the Japanese Navy that hobble into port after battle—ships that may return to sea and endanger our boys." It could accommodate the largest ships afloat.

Cockpit B-29 Superfortress

During the briefing, we were ordered, "*Take it out, blow it to bits, close it down.*'"

Flights to and from our targets depicted not war or death, but the beauty of Southeast Asia, China and even Japan. Despite my hatred for the Japs, I couldn't help but think of them as people. Yet I could not understand their brutality in murdering men, women and children. Besides Peggy—my beautiful redheaded wife—Carl Hansman was the only other person I shared these thoughts with. I'm not sympathetic, I hate the Japs. I just don't understand.

"Confirmed, Duff, that's our turning point to Singapore," Carl answered. Back in Salina, Kansas, Carl and I were trained to know each other's job— bombardier and navigator—in the event one could not carry out his assignment during a mission.

Carl was Peggy's favorite too. Often, Carl joined us for dinner in our "cardboard box," the home the military provided for a married officer and his wife.

It got its name the evening the three of us sat around a makeshift kitchen table dining on a pretty sad steak. Carl was sawing his steak when a leg of his chair broke through the wood floor, dropping him from sight. He took the table and our fine plastic china with him, while Peggy and I sat, holding knife and fork. Laughter complemented dessert.

I am 1st Lt. William Farrell Duffy, or "Duff." I'm twenty-four. I was born and raised in Chicago, Illinois, the oldest of four children—three boys, one girl. Dad was a Chicago cop, which nurtured his lack of softness or sensitivity. Will Duffy, gruff, opinionated and always in control, so he thought. Mom—Mae Doyle—was stiff competition for dominion in the home. When Dad yelled, Mom would shut all the windows, so the neighbors wouldn't hear. When Mom yelled, Dad would open all the windows, so the neighbors could hear.

I found this amusing, until I married. During our courtship, I shared this story with Peggy, and she used it the first time I raised my voice. She opened the windows and folded her arms across her chest, but the grin in her eyes and McCormick smile disarmed me. Our quarrel ended with a kiss.

Our pilot, Major Donald Humphrey, broke in. "Carl, I've got visual also. Elevation 18,000 feet, airspeed 300 MPH."

"Hump, turn her two degrees . . . come to course one-zero-three. We'll pick up the Malaya coastline and be headed for Singapore," Carl directed.

"Turning her two degrees to course one-zero-three," Humphrey confirmed.

Hump had the honor of our airship—*Postville Express*—being named after his hometown, Postville, Iowa, "population minus seventy-four," we teased. Each week Hump was mailed the *Postville Herald* and we took pleasure reading about international and national events taking shape in this hub of the world. Carl and I, plus a few other officers, would tape to our locker clippings from the newspaper, such as: *Marguerite Cunningham had her sisters Marie, Florence, and Ruth Cunningham from Marquette, Iowa, call on her at home this past Saturday. The three enjoyed a delightful meal of fried chicken, followed with homemade ice cream. Afterwards, Marguerite led her guests on a stroll through town, to view our new spillway for the*

Yellow River watershed and our Gazebo.

Hump replied, "You city boys just envy our small town and the fact we know one another by name, and don't rely on bad news to get a paper to press." Funny, but it was true. I grew close to this northeast Iowa community, and would devour the paper each week.

"Duff, you ready to deliver our airmail of one thousand pound bombs to the addressee?" Hump asked.

I was busy fiddling with the Norden bombsight, the Army Air Corp's top-secret instrument. It combined visual aiming with a calculating device, to determine the exact moment for me to release the bombs.

Looking over my left shoulder allowed me to see Hump, sitting above my position in the pilot seat. His long fingers gripped a wheel—shaped like a half moon—to pilot our ship. His brown eyes danced with the gauges on the panel before him, the blue morning sky, and the sea below.

I smiled and responded, "Ready for delivery, Hump. But let's not try to collect the postage due on the Japs' mail. We may find them somewhat irate once it's opened."

Small laughter filled the plane's interphone system. It connected our eleven-man crew by headsets with receivers and transmitters. The most laughter came from the tail gunner, Staff Sgt. Rouhier Spratt, age twenty-seven, from Gilbert, West Virginia.

Spratt's position in the tail of the B-29 was home from beginning until the end of each mission. Cut off from the other men except by interphone, his pressurized compartment in the tail barely allowed room for him. He sat on a leather seat and faced backward to

Postville Express Crew

Back row:
> Major Donald J. Humphrey–Pilot;
> Nelson–copilot (Lt. Col. Billings had his seat);
> Capt. Carl A. Hansman–navigator;
> 1st Lt. William F. Duffy–bombardier;
> 1st Lt. Ernest C. Saltzman–flight engineer;
> 1st Lt. Martin J. Govednik–radar;

Front row:
> T/Sgt. Michael A. Kundrat–radio operator;
> T/Sgt. Harold D. Gillett–left gunner;
> S/Sgt. John A. MacDonald–top gunner;
> T/Sgt. Ralph C. Lindley–right gunner;
> S/Sgt. Rouhier E. Spratt–tail gunner

view encroaching enemy aircraft hoping to attack our rear. Spratt had windows to his left, right and straight ahead. His tools included two .50-caliber machine guns and a 20-mm cannon to discourage visitors.

"Which area of the post office am I working in, Major Humphrey sir," Spratt called.

"Why Spratt, you greet all callers at our back door. A very important job. You watching our back door, Sergeant?"

Spratt's keen eyes and instincts had contributed to destroying two enemy aircraft on previous missions. He was credited for a third, recorded by headquarters as "probably destroyed," since the kill could not be verified by any other airmen. All were brought down during the last two combat missions of the *Postville Express*, at Cheng-Hsien, China, and Omura, Japan. Spratt and a bombardier from another aircraft shared the lead for destroyed enemy craft, yet Spratt had that "probably destroyed" behind his name. The two men led the entire 793d Squadron before this mission.

"Always watching the back door sir!" Spratt called. "I sure like the view to the east." The sun had splashed red and orange across the horizon and the sea. "It's going to be a beautiful day."

"Okay, Spratt, quiet! Use the eyes for the enemy and keep the back door secure," Humphrey ordered.

"Won't let you down, Major!"

"Hump, there's the Malaya coast, at two o'clock," I announced. Mist covered most of the shoreline. The silhouette of the jungle lay beyond. We had knowledge that Chinese Communist guerrillas had been living in the jungle for the past three years, hiding from the

Japanese, who invaded Malaya the very day they attacked Pearl Harbor. It took the Japs just over two months to completely occupy Malaya and Singapore. The British never thought the Japs would attack from the north; it had always been assumed they would come by sea, at Singapore. It was a crushing defeat to Britain and the Allies.

On Humphrey's right was Lt. Col. Robinson Billings, sitting in this morning as copilot. His regular assignment was group operations officer at headquarters, Kharagpur, India. Billings was along to observe the mission and assist or relieve Hump if necessary, but he was not in command. The flight was Humphrey's.

"See the coast, Colonel?" Humphrey asked.

"Yes, it looks peaceful. That will change when we reach Singapore. We'll have everyone awake by then!"

"Radar to pilot!" Lt. Govednik broke in. Marty Govednik, age twenty-five, came from Chisholm, Minnesota, a town of only a few thousand people in the far northern region of the state.

"Go ahead, Marty, what have you got," Humphrey answered.

"Hump, we've got a beauty of a storm ahead and there's no way around it. The good news is, it shouldn't interfere with our target at Singapore. It's already been there, but we may have cloud cover over the target."

"How long will we be in the storm's path?"

"Twenty minutes. Maybe!"

"You see any sign of our squadron on your radar?"

"No, not a one."

"Thanks, Marty, keep me posted."

Humphrey called to Radioman Mick Kundrat.

"Mick, any contact with the other ships?"

"Not a whisper, Hump."

"Okay, I'm breaking radio silence. We need to know their whereabouts."

Eighteen other B-29s made up our squad that morning. Humphrey managed to radio two of them. The others missed our rendezvous, probably headed to the secondary targets we agreed on if there were problems reaching our primary target.

We met the storm and Marty was right—it was a beauty. The clouds were deep gray, almost black in areas, and they stretched across the sky. Lightning bolts cracked toward the sea. We had to fly through it, since its ceiling was too high to fly over. The force pitched our big bird back and forth, shaking it violently.

My stomach was hit by a steep drop in altitude, followed by rocking, then a sudden lift, as if it were a rubber raft on a raging sea. I gripped the edge of my seat and pressed the bottom of my combat boots to the floor. My insides rose and fell.

I was thankful I didn't have the cup of coffee Hump had offered earlier. Strokes of lightning and their thunderclaps were one on top of another. I feared lightning would hit the big aluminum can we were riding in, plummeting our craft into turbulent waters below.

I thought of Peggy and our children, common when danger and death seemed close at hand. It triggered reflection on life, love, family, anything meaningful. I imagined my beautiful redhead, twenty-four years old, mother of two children, and a widow. Our son, Danny, his smile, giggle and beautiful black curls. I had little time to know him before I left for India in the spring of 1944.

I missed his second birthday, September 5, which was discouraging. The combat mission three days later to Anshan, Manchuria, was bad. I had a nightmare before the mission: Our plane was the victim of a *kamikaze* attack. As I sat in the nose of our B-29, I watched a Jap "Tony" close the gap between our two planes. My guns were empty and I could see the Jap pilot smiling as he aimed his ship at our nose. He was laughing at the fear in my eyes. At the moment of the fiery explosion I woke up, wet in perspiration and trembling.

It was on my mind during the Anshan mission. I couldn't shake it until we bombed the target and were headed home. The mission went well. We were in and out with little opposition and the nightmare ended.

One month later I received a telegram. My Peggy delivered a healthy baby girl October 8, baptized Margaret after her mother. It was mid-November before the mail brought me my first picture of Peggy Anne. Tears filled my eyes and a lump pained my throat as I gazed at our beautiful daughter. I sensed the softness of her skin, the smell of powder in her red hair, the tiny lips of her smile, her blue Irish eyes and her gibberish chatter.

"Duff, twelve minutes from target, how are things looking?" Carl radioed from his navigation table.

"Ice on our nose, Carl, I can't see anything yet. We're coming out of the storm though. Hump, can you bring us down, to see if we can shake this ice?"

"I'll try, Duff. The storm carries an updraft. It

Peggy Duffy with Danny & Peggy Anne

shot us from seventeen to twenty-six thousand feet in under two minutes," Humphrey replied.

"Bombardier to radar."

"Go ahead bombardier," Marty answered.

"Marty, the ice has me blind up here. No chance to drop bombs visually if we can't shake it. If not, I'll count on you and your radar to be my eyes."

"Okay, Duff, I'll find the target."

We had lost radio contact with the two remaining craft from our squadron, not a word since before the storm. "Hump, are we on our own?" I asked.

"Yeah, we're no longer the lead plane of our squad, we are the squad!"

"Hump, Col. Billings is observing this morning. So far, we have blistered his butt with an eight-hour flight. We took him into a tropical storm, and lost all eighteen of our B-29 squadron before reaching our target. Are you wondering how his report will read when he gets back to base?" I joked.

"Duff, that's crossed my mind. Wouldn't it be wonderful if you were to bomb the living daylight out of the Japs' dry dock? Then Col. Billings could report: *The Postville Express is by far the most prestigious Superfortress within our family of B-29 bombers. Major Donald Humphrey excused the eighteen-ship formation accompanying him on the Singapore mission and destroyed the enemy target using skill, determination and superior direction.*

Laughter filled the interphone. I looked over my right shoulder at Col. Billings and smiled. He shook his head side to side, then replaced his smile with a determined look and responded in that Boston accent,

"Okay, fly-boys, settle down and show me why we have assigned this crew as squadron leader. I want that floating dry dock turned into a surplus of tooth picks."

In the next minute the crew grew silent and tended to final preparations for the bomb run. Each of us put on flak jacket and helmet, protection from enemy shrapnel and shells that could pierce a cabin wall.

The left-and right-side gunners and top gunner stationed in the waist cabin would swing the double .50-caliber machine gun turrets, check rotation, ensure ammunition was set, and ready the gun sights.

At the tail, Spratt would do the same, swinging the big guns wide, high, low testing for range and mobility.

Ready, all would watch for enemy aircraft through a Plexiglas blister or window at their position.

Each man traveled in thought, reflecting on the treasures in his life today, right now. Family, girlfriend, wife, children, life, death, love, hate, war, peace. All silent, waiting and readying ourselves for what lay ahead.

I thought of my parents, Mae and Will, and their fear and anxiety with two boys at war—my younger brother, Bob, age twenty-two, a glider pilot stationed in Britain, and me.

It was easy to see myself as a boy, with death searching for me and so close at hand. They called us "men," the Air Corps, and maybe this was to prepare us mentally, but sure as shooting, the boy crept his way back into me. I could wear the face of a man—strong, confident, determined—yet dream like a boy.

Before this war, the farthest I had traveled from our home in Chicago was Wisconsin, for Duffy summer vacations. We would rent a cabin on the shore of a spring-fed lake, part of a chain of twenty-eight lakes. Fishing, swimming, boating, the fresh smell of pine trees, and the cushion of fallen needles under your feet.

At night, I would walk to the edge of the dock and sit. Looking out on the glass-like lake, I would break the surface of the water with my bare feet. I would lie back and view millions of stars dotting the sky. I could travel the universe, searching for my destiny. Never did those thoughts take me to this side of the world. Night stars are different over the southern hemisphere, though my dreams never notice.

It's funny how the mind wanders to what seems insignificant, especially just prior to a bombing run or combat with the enemy. Bits and pieces flash before me, and sometimes I hear the small voice, "Is this it, is our number up?"

Eleven bombing missions, twenty-two Himalaya crossings into China, and now mission number twelve. Twenty-six thousand feet above the South China Sea, ready to release four one thousand pound bombs on Singapore.

I will always remember the second mission. It was June 15, 1944, over Yawata, Japan. The mission was called to strike the mainland of Japan, for the first time with the B-29. Its primary purpose was to destroy the coke ovens of Japan's largest steel plant, Imperial Iron and Steel Works, which produced one-fourth of their rolled steel. The other reason was to arouse the American public.

Since December 7, 1941—the Jap surprise attack at Pearl Harbor—our people had had to wait 2½ years for this mission. Hitting the Japanese homeland showed their vulnerability, and it renewed the fire and confidence that the United States needed to defeat these aggressors.

Seventy-five planes were to make the mission. One crashed and burned on takeoff, but the crew escaped. Six B-29s aborted takeoff, four turned back early in the mission, leaving sixty-four heading for Japan. Only forty-seven found the target at 11:38 p.m. China time. Searchlights stabbed the silver bodies of our B-29s as we flew over the blackout city. The *Postville Express* was the first over the target, making me the first bombardier during World War II to drop bombs on Japan from a B-29.

What a tribute . . . such an honor . . . I was very proud. I thought of Pearl Harbor and the more than 2,300 lives lost when the Japs attacked our boys that early Sunday morning, sinking battleships USS *Arizona*, *Oklahoma*, *California*, *Nevada* and *West Virginia*, damaging three other battleships, inflicting major damage on three cruisers and three destroyers, along with destroying two hundred U.S. planes. Well, this was the beginning of our presence at Japan's door, and we planned to make ourselves regular visitors. Our second attack. . . .

I was jerked from my daydream by an enemy attack. Jap fighters greeted our advancing B-29.

Four minutes from our Singapore target, Humphrey had managed to bring the large bird down to twenty-three thousand feet. This was the most vulnerable time of the mission. The ship had to maintain an uninterrupted course, so I could carry out my task

    During the flight the bombardier–Duffy–was responsible for climbing down into the two bomb bay sections of the B-29 to activate each bomb by pulling its pin. This task occurred only after lift-off to avoid blowing themselves up in the event they crashed on takeoff.

as bombardier. All the while, fighters came at us with blazing machine guns. I had to ignore the attacking force and concentrate on the target. The flight here was eight hours, with the trip home yet to come, but the success of our mission depended on these few minutes.

I ran over final calculations and adjusted the bombsight. The bomb bay doors were lowered. Humphrey passed control of the *Postville Express* to me and I piloted the plane toward the target. Through the Norden bombsight, I piloted our bomber according to calculations and instructions from radar, and held the heading as we neared the target.

Fighter attacks increased, hitting at our nose, but I forced myself to ignore their pursuit and concentrate on my target. Sweat beaded on my forehead and rolled toward my eyes. A swipe with my shirtsleeve soaked them up.

Any moment now . . . Steady Bill . . . Thoughts on the target . . . Be patient, let it happen . . . Perspiration beneath my khaki flight suit dampened my tee shirt and sent a chill down my back and underarms. I wiped moisture from my hands on the cotton covering my thighs and returned to the knobs of the bombsight. My body prepared for battle.

Our gunners were busy with no fewer than fifteen Jap fighter attacks in one minute. "Zekes," "Tonys" and "Oscars" filled the sky, diving sometimes three at a time. Antiaircraft artillery fire dotted the sky and rocked our ship. The racket of the guns faded inside my head as I concentrated on the target and radar's direction.

It was 8:54 a.m., January 11, 1945, when I yelled, *"Bombs away!"*

I returned control of the plane to Humphrey, and for the next sixty seconds, he held the ship on course, to let the automatic camera record hits on the target. The flash of exploding bombs triggered the camera to shoot pictures, used by intelligence to assess damage to the target. With the pictures taken, Humphrey turned our ship sharp right, to get us out of there and head home.

"Duff, any sight of the target? Were you on?" Hump asked.

"Hump, I was blind! Let's pray the radar had good eyes and the settings were correct," I answered.

"Pilot to tail gunner!"

"Spratt here, Major!"

"Can you see the target, Spratt?"

"Negative, Major, cloud cover."

"Damn!"

"Maybe the cameras will pick it up, Hump," I offered.

"Yeah, maybe."

With Hump in control of the ship, I focused on the Jap fighters coming in at our nose. The sound of gunfire and aerial bombs was strong. Enemy planes stayed with us and now numbered thirty-five, perhaps forty. Most aimed their attack at the nose of our bomber, high and level, very coordinated, coming head-on, firing all the way. Just as they reached us, they would roll over and dive underneath and continue firing at the belly of our B-29. But they didn't seem to be hitting us, or at least where it counted.

Lindley, right gunner, hit our first one. He called over the interphone, "Got one. He's on fire and falling fast toward the Strait of Malacca. I'm tracking another in my gun sight, it's diving under the wing. Damn, he got away!"

Our burst of .50-caliber guns, targeting Jap fighters crossing our path, continued nonstop. Above, fighters dropped aerial bombs, and explosions shook our B-29 violently. There was no relief as we retreated up the west coast of Malaya. The fighters staged attacks from all sides, working us over repeatedly.

Spratt phoned as he was yacking with the tail guns, "I have the rear closed off. Dishing it out pretty good to visitors. Oh boy, got a Zeke, diving on my right, he'll be with you next, Gillett," he called to the left gunner. "I'm swinging on him, with a dose of .50-caliber lead." His voice grew louder. "One hundred yards . . . seventy-five . . . fifty . . . I hit it . . . It's falling apart, pieces of fire everywhere!" Spratt added.

When Spratt was not providing updates, there was plenty of chatter phoned from the waist cabin gunners Gillett, Lindley and MacDonald. They were burning up the sky with the constant blare of the two heavy guns, within each revolving turret, picking out the most threatening of the attacking force, while others were ignored.

With the thunderstorm behind us, the sky opened up a sea of blue. We continued up the coast, climbing in altitude and speed, hoping to shake the Jap fighters.

In the nose, I was firing on an Oscar head-on, till it dove beneath the ship. My eyes picked up another, high at eleven o'clock, firing its guns in a steady stream as it advanced on our ship. I wiped sweat from my brow, lined up the Oscar in my gun sight and returned the fire.

Aerial bombs continued to fall on us, shaking and tossing the big bird. The fighter plane's determination in its attack, coming straight in without altering its course, worried me. I recalled other American bombers under such attack, ending with the enemy ramming their ship, creating a fiery explosion, and death to the crew.

My stomach got queasy, and throat dry, while I tracked the enemy in the gun sight and flooded its path with .50-caliber bullets. It lasted forever, it seemed. During a fight, I tended to think of the exchange of shells between the enemy and me, knowing that one of us might connect and hit the other. My heartbeat increased and I tensed in the long moments. There is no way to get by these thoughts, it was going to happen. I could only hope I was better than the guy behind the other guns.

I got him . . . scored a hit. The Oscar exploded, shooting a bright yellow and orange fire across the sky, briefly engulfing the nose of our B-29. Large and small pieces of the enemy craft scattered and dropped to the sea. Tension eased and my stomach started to feel better, but I was chilled by more perspiration in my clothes.

The crew had faced tight spots before and always come through with only scratches. But we were facing more than double the number of enemy fighters than we had encountered on previous missions. Plus, we had always been in the company of other B-29s from our squad, which helped the odds—but now we were battling the attackers alone.

.50 caliber machine gun shell recovered
from the crash site of the B-29 *Postville Express.*

Another Oscar challenged, coming head-on, spraying firepower ahead of it. I returned the fire, as the distance between our ships disappeared. I hit it and a stream of black smoke followed the enemy's tail, as it passed under the right wing. I called to the right waist gunner, "Lindley, finish off the Oscar, at four o'clock!"

"You took care of him, Duff. He's falling to the sea!"

I spotted a Tony high at one o'clock, about nine hundred yards out, firing continually and closing the gap fast. Swinging my guns on the diving plane, I fired constantly. The fighter never swerved, coming in over our heads, passing within fifty feet.

The blast of a shell penetrated the top of the Plexiglas nose, stirring dust about the cabin. Piercing cold air rushed in, dropping the air pressure and sounding the warning klaxon for the crew to put on oxygen masks.

"Pilot to crew, get your oxygen masks on, repeat, get your masks on!" Humphrey yelled over the phone.

I put my mask to my face and attached it behind my head, then looked over my right shoulder to locate the moaning voice that accompanied the whistle of air in the cabin. Colonel Billings had been hit, left thigh, his pants saturated with red. He was conscious, attaching an oxygen mask to his strained face. A hole in the Plexiglas above Billings' head showed the path of the destructive shell. Humphrey noticed also and questioned him.

"Colonel, are you all right?"

Billings nodded yes and said with a snicker, "Hope

I don't lose that leg, it's a damn good leg."

Humphrey called Kundrat, "Mick, get up here with the first aid kit, the colonel has been hit!"

In my left ear resounded the stomp of Humphrey's foot on the rudder control pedal. He hollered to Billings, who was holding his leg tight in both hands. "Colonel, have you got any rudder? Try your controls!"

Billings sat forward, made contact with his foot, then shook his head no to Humphrey. Mick, kneeling beside him, tended his leg.

As the excitement behind me continued, I saw another fighter plane coming head on, at twelve o'clock high. Swiveling the gun sight, I took aim and tracked the invader perfectly, pointing the forward turrets, holding six .50-caliber guns, at the fuselage of the craft. Confident with my aim, I engaged the guns to blast it to pieces and send it to join the other Jap ships in the sea.

The big guns didn't fire. They tracked the target, but no firepower. Holding the guns on the enemy fighter, I tried again. Each attempt yielded nothing. I prayed as I pretended to shoot the guns, hoping to make the enemy believe it was under fire.

"Hump, my guns are out. I'm not getting anything. I can swing on them, but no fireworks!"

"Major, this is Lindley. My guns are silent too!"

The same reports came in from Gillett, and MacDonald. The central fire control system that operated all the guns except the tail station was inoperative. That last "Tony" did the damage.

There was a drop and tilt in the plane's course. Humphrey and I glanced at each other. Looking out windows on both sides of the plane, we could see each of the four Wright Cyclone 2,200-hp engines, each powering a sixteen-foot-diameter propeller. It was the number two engine. The propeller had stopped and the engine housing was torn by enemy shells. Humphrey called to the flight engineer, Ernest Saltzman, "Saltz, kill number two engine!"

Saltzman, seated back to back with the copilot, was out of his chair delivering sulfa powder to the colonel for his wound. He flipped the powder to Mick and jumped back in his seat, grabbing the control and killing the engine.

"Hump, number two shut down!" Saltzman reported.

"Saltz, how far can we fly on three engines?"

"I'll get back to you, I need to do some calculating."

"Duff, any change with the guns?" Humphrey asked.

"Nothing, Hump, we're a sitting duck, nowhere to hide. I have a Tony in my sight and I'm pointing the gun barrels on him, but I think he knows our guns are out!"

Between attacks I removed my hands from the sight and rubbed warmth into them. The high altitude air, blowing into the cabin, was icy. Grabbing the gun sight, I aimed at one of two more fighters making a run on us. It was frightening to sit behind the Plexiglas nose and watch the enemy take turns unloading their firepower on our ship.

"Here come three more Tonys Hump!" I shouted. The diving fighters opened their guns all the way in, riddling our giant Superfortress unopposed. The bursting shells frightened me. Oh, how I wished to take a crack at them!

"Major, number three engine is on fire!" Lindley shouted from right gunner position.

Humphrey and I looked through the window and saw the engine wrapped in flames. We looked at one another, not saying a word. We needed that engine to get home, and close to twenty-eight hundred gallons of hundred octane gasoline were carried in that wing.

"Saltz, feather number three and put out the fire. We need that engine back!" Humphrey ordered.

"Okay, Hump!" Saltzman feathered number three, and put out the blaze using the fire extinguisher built into the engine.

"Hump, I've got those calculations. We can't make it home, but we can ditch the plane at sea in a safe zone and be picked up by submarine. But we need three engines to get to the safe zone!"

"Hump, there's two B-29s at eleven o'clock, about four miles ahead of us!" I hollered. Sight of them lessened my fear and the rising doubt of our return home. It was a beautiful sight.

"Saltz, I need power to catch up to the others. How is number three engine?" Humphrey asked.

"The fire is out, Hump, but a trail of black smoke streaks behind her!"

"Start up number three engine, Saltz, and give me all you can!"

"Bringing number three back up, Hump!"

"Mick, radio our boys ahead of us, let them know we're on their tail and we have engine trouble!" Humphrey shouted.

"Hump, the radio is dead! I've been checking it over, but I haven't found the problem. I'll keep at it and keep you posted."

Suddenly, I realized it was quiet! I searched the sky, and then called for MacDonald in the waist cabin. "Mac, any sign of fighters?"

"Nothing here, Duff! We were just wondering if that was the last of them."

"They're going home!" Spratt called in from the tail section. "Heading back to Singapore!"

Jubilant voices rocked the interphone, until Humphrey announced, "Okay, that's enough, keep the phone open!"

"Radar to pilot!" Marty called.

"What's up, Marty?"

"Hump, we've lost our radar, its gone! I can't get any readings!"

"Work on it, Marty. We have visual of two of our squad ahead of us, so we have someone to follow!"

I turned to look at Billings and nodded to Humphrey to do the same. Billings was lying back; his head tilted left, eyes tightly closed. The bleeding from his thigh seem to have slowed, by the bandaging Mick had wrapped around the leg. His left hand held the wound tight in attempt to relieve the pain.

"Colonel, how are you doing?"

"I'm in bad pain, but I'll be okay. I don't think I'll be much help to you, Hump."

"That's fine, just hang in there."

"Number three engine started, Hump!" Saltzman announced. Silence filled the cabin as we watched the engine. Without three engines our chance for reaching a safe zone was impossible. The propeller turned and quickly came to life, gaining speed until it matched the power of the remaining two engines. The tension within me eased, as I watched it reach full power and operate fine.

In moments it burst into flames. The fire engulfed the engine, covering the wing, and creating a tail behind it.

Saltz called out, "Hump, the flames are worse on number three! I've tried to extinguish them, but it's no use, it's out of control. It's feeding off the fuel tank and it can blow up any moment!"

"Try to give us some time Saltz, do what you can!" Humphrey turned the plane toward the Malayan coast, roughly thirty miles north of the city of Malacca.

He announced over the interphone to the crew, "This is the pilot. Number two engine is out and number three is burning up. I'm heading us to the mainland, where we will bail out over the jungle. We've been briefed that in a situation like this, we should try to establish contact with the Chinese Communist guerrillas. They will be our best chance for survival of the Japs and the jungle.

"Check your parachutes, they should include your jungle survival pack, and make sure you have your Webb belt around your waist. Keep an eye out for one another, so you have an idea where others are touching down. Once we hit the jungle floor, it will be impossible to see each other, so we need to get our bearings before hand. Don't go shouting for one another, because we have no way of knowing if the Japs will be waiting. We'll push east, deeper into the jungle, and hope for a rendezvous. This may be the last time we see each other. I don't know what to say. I haven't rehearsed anything. Good luck. May God be with us!"

Silence swallowed the interphone.

Humphrey turned his attention to our advance. "Duff, we need to avoid open areas and get ourselves into the hill country. Keep an eye out for us."

"Will do, Hump!" I bit down on my lip, while studying the approaching coast. I thought of the times I rehearsed this scene in my head. Shot from the sky, parachuting into Jap-occupied territory, thousands of miles from the base, food, water, Peggy and the children. What's in the jungle . . . Can I survive what's ahead . . . Can a submarine rescue us . . . Can we get word to headquarters.

"Mick, any change in the radio?"

"No! I don't get anything, Hump!"

"Waist and tail section get ready! Open the rear door and await my order to bail out."

Their exit was in the rear storage compartment, the same side as the burning engine. Spratt announced that he was climbing forward from the tail compartment and Marty phoned he was opening the bulkhead door to the storage compartment.

"All standing by, Hump! Spratt, Gillett, MacDonald and Lindley," Marty reported.

The nose cabin was getting hot and the flames from number three engine were streaking nearly fifty yards. Our exit was through the front wheel well. Carl stood up from the navigation table and called, "I've got the hatch!" bending over and lifting a panel in the cabin floor. Humphrey lowered the wheels and said,

The Postville Express' Last Flight

100 MILES

SONGKHLA

SIAM

SATUL

Bay of
Bengal

CALCUTTA TO SINGAPORE
1900 MILES

South
China Sea

KOTA BHARU

PENANG

REDANG

ROUTE OF PLANE

TURNING POINT
TO SINGAPORE

RENDEZVOUS
POINT

CONFINED
IN THIS AREA

MALAY STATES

IPOH

KA LIPIS

TENGGOL

HIT
STORM
AREA

KUANTAN

BAILED OUT
OF BURNING
PLANE

PEKAN

KUALA LUMPUR

HIT BY
FIGHTERS

MERSING

TAMPIN

MALACCA

SUMATRA

PLANE
CAUGHT FIRE
IN CHASE AFTER
TWO PLANES

DROPPED
BOMBS ON
FLOATING
DRYDOCK

BENGKATIS

SINGAPORE

"Stand by in the nose cabin!"

I adjusted and tightened the straps to my parachute, and saw that the ripcord was in place to release the silk canopy.

"Radar to pilot!"

"Go ahead, Marty."

"Hump, we just opened the rear hatch and the sky is a wall of fire! Flames streak from the wing to beyond the tail. Can Saltz give us any relief by killing the fire on that engine?"

I watched as Humphrey turned to Saltzman for an update and saw him shake his head no. "Negative, Marty!"

I called to Humphrey, "You feel that? The shake, the vibration! She's ready to break up."

Humphrey shook his head in agreement.

"Pick your spot, Hump, we have good jungle ahead!" I added.

"Okay, get ready to jump, Duff!"

"Colonel, let's go, let me help you," I said to Billings, grabbing him by the arm to lift him from his seat.

"Thanks, Lieutenant!"

"This is it, when I give the order everyone out, no delays!" Hump announced.

Then came a startling crack, followed by ripping metal and a loud "whoosh," as the right wing tore away from the fuselage. The Superfortress flipped on its right side, tossing us about the nose cabin.

Each man battled to reach the hatch, crawling to the opening of the disintegrating ship. First to jump was Saltzman, followed by Carl. Both made the jump without any event.

I was next to reach the exit. The toss of the bomber hurled my body against the gearing of the wheels. The blow pierced my chest, knocking the wind from me. As I gasped for air, pain shot through my chest, and I felt lightheaded. I took short breaths, feeding my brain needed oxygen, to remain conscious.

The silver wedding band on my finger was caught on a jagged piece of metal. Warm blood covered my hand and wrist. Pulling the finger cut the ring deep into the flesh, yet allowed me leeway to slide the ring off the sharp metal. Free, I pulled my body clear and plunged into the open sky.

Body weight and gear added speed to descent. Before pulling the parachute ripcord, I had to make sure I was clear of the airplane. Then I thought, "What if the chute fails to open?" My mind raced, imagining my last moments. I plummeted toward the ground. I wondered if I would feel pain before I died. I hoped not.

The air turbulence and pressure against my body flattened and tore at my clothes, and prickled my flesh like wind-driven sand.

There was fire and debris all over the sky. I allowed myself to fall about two thousand feet, freeing me from the disintegrating ship and flaming gasoline. Only then did I pull the cord to the parachute. The white silk streamed above me, mushrooming into a canopy of trapped air. It jerked my body to a stop, followed by gentle side-to-side rocking as I floated toward the jungle.

The pain in my chest was agonizing, making

breathing difficult. I guessed a broken rib, on the left side, maybe a punctured lung. The scrapes and bruises were minor. I had made it out of the plane.

I searched the sky and counted parachutes. I spotted six, mine made seven. Four were missing. I looked for enemy fighters, then the jungle floor for Jap troops, who could pick me off with a rifle as I dangled helpless.

I took an inventory of gear. First, the .45-caliber handgun, hanging under my left arm in its shoulder holster. Webb belt with ammunition, canteen, knife, and medical kit. And the jungle survival kit attached to the parachute harness.

Except for a rippling breeze against the silk chute, for the first time in over eight hours I was surrounded by silence in the early morning sky. It was peaceful, settling, despite the danger awaiting as I floated toward the jungle floor.

Talib

In the final moments I gauged where some of the men would land for a rendezvous. Everyone was spread out, and I couldn't tell who was who. I planned to travel east, pushing deeper into the jungle.

I touched down on prickly grass about knee high within a small clearing. Pain shot through my upper body when I hit the ground. It felt like a knife lodged in my chest and I could hardly breathe. I lay on the thistlelike grass, taking short breaths while I pressed both hands against my chest. The pain eased enough that I was able to stand, allowing me to remove the parachute harness.

Behind me, a rustling noise in the bushes frightened me. I turned, gripping the butt of my handgun in one motion. I faced a Malay native, wearing a white loincloth and holding a long machete. His smile eased my tension, but I continued to aim the gun at the thin man's chest.

When he spoke, I could hear only jumbled words. He pointed at the white silk draped over the grass and bushes. The little man held out his hand, jabbering and bowing his head. I nodded yes, lowered the gun and finished the release of the harness from my body, allowing it to fall free.

I extended my hand and presented the prized gift to the brown man. I said, "Can you help me?" His wrinkled forehead and squinting eyes answered. I tried again. "American . . . I am American!"

I poked a finger against my chest, speaking loudly and expressively, as if he would understand better. The native displayed a smile and shook his head yes. Gathering the parachute, he turned and disappeared into the bushes.

I was not sure what his smile meant: "Yes, I'll get you help" or "Yes, you are American and thanks for the parachute." I decided to give him ten minutes, and then move on to locate the others.

I sat with my back against a tree at the spot my new friend had entered the jungle. Using my handkerchief, I wiped blood off my hand and wrist, revealing a deep cut and swelling around my wedding band. On the palm side the ring cut into the flesh until it met bone and I could barely see it. An inch-long gash on the topside revealed torn flesh and protruding bone covered in blood. The throbbing finger approached twice its size. There was no way for me to remove the ring—it would have to wait. I settled for wrapping the finger in gauze and leaned back to rest.

My right hand gripped the butt of the revolver, my index finger stroking the trigger as it lay in my lap.

My left hand massaged my chest, easing the discomfort of my injury.

The chatter of birds and creatures was startling, but it replaced the fear and anxiety I had felt only moments earlier. Resting, I lowered my eyelids and breathed the humid air. My thoughts turned to the battle: wailing engines on the Jap fighters and their constant attack. The rat-a-tat-tat of machine gun shells. Our loss of firepower and how I sat there pretending to shoot them as they took turns trying to down the Superfortress. The final minutes as the *Postville Express* ripped apart and scattered debris across the sky. Humbled today by our demise as many crews in the past. . . .

I was alarmed by movement in the bushes across the clearing. Jumping to my feet, I stood beside the tree, ready to run. With my thumb I pulled back the hammer of the .45 and aimed toward the sound. Was it a Jap search party? How many of them . . . Should I run . . . Shoot . . . Let them take me prisoner . . . I decided to fight.

The bushes parted and Lindley entered the clearing.

"Lindley, you scared me to death!" I eased the gun hammer back to its seat.

"Am I glad to see you, Duff! I didn't know if I would find anyone. I lost my survival kit. Got it caught in the tree I snagged when I landed!" Lindley jabbered. He tripped, his large frame crashing, face down, at my feet. He rolled over on his back and moaned.

"Lindley, you're burned bad! Your face, neck,

hands . . . What happened?"

He spoke slowly, catching his breath along the way. "When we opened our hatch, there was a wall of fire from the wing . . . The wing ripped away and we all started jumping . . . Spratt went first . . . You could hear him screaming as he fell . . . It was terrible!

"After a few moments Mac, then Gillett, jumped. I think they timed a break in the flames . . . Anyway, I didn't hear them yell like Spratt. I was next . . . I guess I got the same dose as Spratt. The vapor stuck to me till it burned itself out. I was scared the parachute would burn and I would fall to the ground!

"Govednick was behind me. I know he made it. I saw his chute for a few minutes. The others made it too, but I lost them. My eyelids got burned and my eyes were stinging. They watered up and everything looked blurry. I can see pretty good now, but the eyelids sting something fierce!"

The skin of his hands, face and neck was charred black or seared off, exposing tissue that seeped blood and precious fluid. His eyebrows and eyelashes were gone and the brown hair on his head was singed short. I opened Lindley's first aid kit and applied ointment, hoping to keep infection down, then wrapped gauze around the hands and neck. There was little I could do for him. He would have to wait until we reached safety.

"Duff, any idea where the others landed?"

"A few came down east of here probably within a half mile. I counted six chutes plus mine." Just then noise to our left signaled an intruder.

"Lindley, get up quick!" I whispered. "Stay beside

the tree but be prepared to make a run for the jungle. I'll give the order." I wiped sweat from my brow before it reached my eyes, then rubbed the moist hand across my chest irritating the ring finger. My throat was dry and it was hard to swallow as we waited. Our guns were cocked and aimed at the approaching sound. A hand parted the large green leaves of the bush and a person stepped into the clearing.

"Whoa! It's me, Saltzman. Hold your fire!"

Saltzman was badly burned too. I cringed at the sight of his black, oozing skin. Their pain had to be overwhelming. I was glad I had my injuries and not theirs.

Saltzman told how he landed in a tree, swung his body to the trunk, and climbed down, falling the last twenty-five feet to the ground. His right hand tore the burned flesh from the back of his left as he clutched them together to escape the fall, leaving him with a palm of skin. He had patched himself up with his first aid kit and started out to find the others.

I told Saltzman and Lindley about the Malay native and my parachute.

"Saltz, take a few minutes' rest. We'll stay here and see how my friend does. If he doesn't show in ten minutes we'll head out and look for the others."

We didn't wait long when a young Malay boy, barefoot and wearing a loincloth, joined us in the clearing. He spoke broken English, and got across to us that if we walked back up the trail we would find other Americans.

The boy led and I followed. Lindley was next and Saltzman watched our rear. Thick vegetation lined both sides, obstructing our view beyond eight to ten feet. Bushes, plants and trees hid each turn of the trail and what might lie ahead. Leaves on some bushes or short trees were the size of an elephant's ear.

"Slow, young man!" I cautioned the boy. His bony appearance, and that of the man earlier, suggested that the Malay diet was not too substantial.

In minutes we found a parachute harness, jungle survival kit and rubber life vest lying on the trail. The name "HANSMAN" was printed on the vest.

"Carl's gear!" I whispered. "He must have been captured."

"This could be a trap, Duff!" Lindley warned.

"Hey, the kid is gone," I said. The boy had vanished into the jungle.

"Duff, that kid may be delivering us to the Japs," Saltzman said. "I don't like the looks of this!"

"We'll stay on this trail and take it slow and easy. Keep your eyes and ears open!" I instructed. Grabbing Carl's survival kit, I swung it over my shoulder with my own pack. I threw the life vest and harness into the bushes, out of sight.

Despite the pain and discomfort of our injuries we moved on, concentrating on what lay ahead. The morning heat and humidity dampened our flight suits with sweat. The jungle racket of birds and hidden animals kept us on edge as we cautiously followed the trail, our eyes tracking each stirring as we moved slowly.

In ten minutes the jungle thinned and opened to a large clearing. On the far side, maybe thirty yards, was the burning fuselage of our destroyed B-29. Black and gray smoke rolled toward the blue sky.

Surely this would show the Japs our location.

About thirty people were gathered, watching it burn—all eager to see the American bomber. Each dressed in a mish-mash of clothing. One man wore a yellow suit that appeared to be silk; another wore a soiled white suit. But most wore clothes that were odds and ends of shabby, unfitted pieces. A few were in loincloths. It was obvious their clothes were meant for comfort or protection, rather than style. About six of the men had rifles in their hands or over their shoulders, and stood close together.

Suddenly the native boy appeared alongside us. I was through playing with this kid and stuck my .45 in his back and motioned for him to step forward. Unsure what the group would do, I slowly proceeded into the clearing. All eyes were on us and the boy.

"Duff, someone is coming!" Saltzman warned. With guns in hand, he and Lindley took a position on either side of the trail leading to the clearing.

I was in the open, fifteen feet from the trailhead. I had sight of the trail and the group gathered at the wreck. I kept my .45 on the boy. I placed my left hand on his shoulder to hold him still, pointed the gun at his temple and used his small frame as a shield. He would be our protection, I hoped. I knew I couldn't shoot the boy, but I prayed the newcomers and the others believed I would.

I glanced at Lindley and Saltzman aiming their guns, then at the group gathered at the fuselage, particularly the men with the rifles talking among themselves. The odds were not good—except we had the element of surprise, if that counted for anything.

We were quiet as the intruders neared. The seconds passed slowly.

I looked at Lindley. The burns sent a chill racing along my spine. His face was growing worse with time. Beet red, puffy and patches where the skin was burnt black or raw. If he turned his head he used his whole upper body to avoid stretching the painful skin of his neck. His left hand hung at his side while the right was stretched around the butt of his gun. I shifted my view to Saltzman. His face wasn't as bad, but otherwise he was a carbon copy of Lindley. We were some force to reckon with.

Two persons appeared. To our delight, it was Humphrey and Hansman.

"Hump . . . Carl!" Saltzman called. "Am I glad to see you!"

"You two okay?" Hump asked Lindley and Saltzman.

Both men nodded yes despite the terrible burns.

"How about you, Duff?"

"I'm all right, Hump!" I lowered my .45 and pointed it at the young boy's back. "How about you two?"

"I landed in a tree about sixty feet from the ground. If not for Carl I never would have gotten down," Humphrey said. "What's going on here?"

Humphrey and Carl were brought up to date on the latest developments.

"Any idea where the others are?" I asked.

"We haven't seen anyone," Humphrey said.

"I saw seven chutes open up including mine." I reported.

"I counted eight." Humphrey said.

"Did Billings or Mick get out?"

"Billings jumped ahead of me, but I don't know about Mick."

"We all know how Mick felt about jumping into Jap territory. Still, I hope he had second thoughts and made the jump," I said. "Billings was in pretty sad shape before we lost the right wing."

"Yeah, he was hurting bad!"

I was standing with the boy, separate from the rest of the crew, when a small man among the natives broke out in a loud jabber. All eyes and guns turned toward this brown-skinned native, who was dressed in trousers too small, a shirt too large, a velvet hat, and what appeared to be a woman's discarded bolero jacket.

He screamed at the men huddled with their rifles in hand. Slowly, they stepped back with the other natives and lowered their weapons. The little man turned his attention to the five of us and the boy, and proceeded toward us. A younger man, barefoot and dressed in a long white nightgown, followed him.

We spread out and pointed our revolvers at this daring man. I sensed our boys behind me backing me up. The man came within two feet of me before he stopped, removed his hat and bowed. He straightened up, displayed a big smile and said, "Good morning, Tuan!" in an Oxford accent.

The accent surprised me and I know it showed on my face. I bowed my head and said, "Can you hide us from the Japs?"

Again the man smiled and motioned for us to follow him. He led us back into the jungle to the same trail we came on. I glanced for the last time at the burning fuselage of the *Postville Express*. She had carried us safely from Kansas to India, across the Himalayas and to and from our targets. The security I had felt flying high in the sky, protected by .50-caliber machine guns, was reduced to a .45-caliber pistol, the jungle and an unknown future in Jap-occupied Malaya.

The boy I had used as a hostage watched as we made our departure. I gave a smile and saluted him. He grinned and bowed his head in return.

"What is your name?" Hump asked our Malay friend.

"Talib," the little man answered. "I am headman of Kampong Kota and that is my son." He pointed to the young man in the nightgown, whom he instructed to run on ahead to be our lookout. Talib was joined by a friend named Samsudin, a Malay lad about twenty-two years old, married only one week earlier. Their courage and compassion in spite of the danger they faced was remarkable, for if the Japs found out their punishment was death.

"Have you seen any other Americans?" Hump asked. "Six men are missing!"

"No! I have not seen other men. I only heard loud explosion and I run to see with the others," Talib said. "You were only men to come to airplane. Perhaps they will find other friendly Malay. Maybe Communist Chinese!"

"Can you take us to the Communist Chinese?"

"Yes, but first you must hide. It is not safe here, many Japanese soldiers will come!"

"Talib, where are we?" I pulled a silk map of the Malaya Peninsula from my pack and showed it to him, with Hump and Carl looking on.

"Tampin, eight kilometers south. Seremban, twenty kilometers north. We are three kilometers west of road that travels between two towns. This is problem, because many Japanese soldiers. Tampin, three hundred Japs. Seremban, eight hundred Japs. They will come for you!" Talib warned.

Hump, Carl and I looked at each other without speaking. Saltzman and Lindley were becoming a handful. The burns lowered their concentration and we had to lead them at times.

For the next two hours we moved fast over rugged trails in the dense jungle. Tree, vine, plant and bushes prevented any breeze on the jungle floor and hampered travel. It was difficult to breathe the humid air. Flight suits wet with perspiration stuck to our bodies. If the journey wasn't hot and sticky, it was chilly and damp.

Talib told us that the men with the rifles at the crash site were Malay police recruited by the Japanese to serve in rural areas. He explained, "They are fearful to fight and fearful not to fight. They have been threatened and named traitors by their people. We cooperate with them, make it appear to Japanese they do their job. I told them, 'Americans our friends and we must help them!'"

What a blessing we should link up with Talib and Samsudin.

By early afternoon, Talib had led us away from the trail along a ravine disappearing into thick growth. This connected to a smaller ravine about ten feet

square, where he instructed us to lie down and keep
absolutely quiet. We were only fifty feet from the trail,
which would be covered with Jap soldiers in the hours
ahead. Talib would return after dark.

We collapsed on a bed of grass, weeds and mud.
It was not comfortable and it had a swamplike odor
to it. This low area probably filled with runoff from
the rugged terrain surrounding it. It didn't matter. Just
to stop and rest made me happy.

Saltzman's and Lindley's burns were irritated by
their clothes and perspiration stinging the burned
flesh. We tended to the burns the best we could, but
the first aid kits provided minimal supplies to work
with. There was morphine, but we decided that if we
had to move out quickly, the men had to be ready—
not drugged. Also, we needed to save it in case there
were more serious injuries. After the medical attention
Saltzman and Lindley pretty much passed out.

"Carl, Hump, I need some help. You got to get
my wedding ring off this finger!" I held the left hand
out for them to view the torn and swollen finger.

"Yeah, we got to get that off you or you'll lose the
finger!" Hump said.

"I've had time to think this through. All we have
is our knife. I can place my hand on a rock or branch
so it will push the ring up and away from the skin.
Then, you cut through the ring, not the finger!" I
smiled. "Who wants the honor?" I asked.

"I'll be happy to do it, Duff. If I screw up, well
then we'll score it Carl ten and Duffy nine, but you
keep the finger!"

"You're a sick, sick man Carl Hansman! You'll

have to face Peggy and explain your stupidity, you know. She likes the fingers!" The three of us laughed until Carl started the cut. Hump held my hand in place and Carl made one-way slices with the blade. It wasn't too bad. They had the ring off pretty quick and the finger felt better.

"Took you a hell of a lot longer to get this ring on, Duff! Wasn't it your parents who offered Peggy money to say yes?" Carl joked. The laughter returned and we disturbed Lindley's sleep. Clean and bandaged, I had only to contend with the throbbing pain in the finger. I tucked the ring in a buttoned pocket for safekeeping. "I will get it repaired when I get home," I assured myself.

"What do you guys think of Talib?" Hump asked. He leaned his six-foot frame against a wall of the ravine and removed his boots.

"I like the man," I replied. "He put on quite the show back there with the natives, and took care of the Malay police nicely." Carl and I took notice of the foot massage Hump had started on his bare foot, and followed his lead.

"He could bring the Japs back," Hump said. "We're at his mercy!"

"Yeah, we are. But we can't move around on our own, either!" Carl said. "We have no idea where we're at or where we're going. We have to trust him!" Carl combed his fingers through his brown hair, releasing a beetle that he swat at and missed.

"He's our only prayer, Hump," I said.

We took inventory. For five men, we had four jungle survival kits. Each contained a machete, leather

1st Lt. William Duffy and Capt. Carl Hansman
Kharagpur, India 1944

gloves, rain poncho, silk map of Malaya, compass, matches, sewing kit, fishing line and hook, one meal ration kit and malted milk tablets, mosquito head net, insect repellent—which the bugs enjoyed—a rope, a book on *How to Survive in the Jungle* which proved useless, and a Chinese-English pocket book of words and phrases.

Each man had his Webb belt—canteen, ammunition pouch, knife and sheath, and medical kit—an Army Air Corp-issued leather flight jacket, khaki flight suit and boots. Between us, we had five .45-caliber handguns and a total of 140 shells.

Our gear was adequate. You wouldn't want to carry more in this heat and humidity. We carried Saltz's pack, but Lindley's was lost with his parachute.

I tried to sleep in the afternoon and evening, but was jumpy. The continual cackle and chatter of jungle creatures unnerved Hump, Carl and me.

The morning events played over in my head. The air battle, buckling of the right wing, our struggle to bail out, the fuselage wreckage and our missing buddies—Marty, Billings, Spratt, Mick, Gillett, and MacDonald.

This led to new concerns: Japs, Talib, jungle, heat, food and injuries. A cloud covered my thoughts, blurring certainty.

I drifted to Peggy, the most beautiful woman in my world. Our blind date for her high school dance, the flaming red hair and disposition to match, but mostly her beauty and love. She taught me about love.

In the days ahead, a Western Union telegram would arrive for Peggy from the War Department stating, "*The Secretary of War desires me to express his deep regret that your husband First Lieutenant William F. Duffy has been reported missing in action since 11 January 1945 in India-Burma area. If further details or other information are received you will be promptly notified.*"

Back in Chicago, neighbors, friends, and relatives learned to fear the sight of the Western Union carrier bicycling up the street. No one expected good news in a telegram. It was a luxury to send or receive one, so naturally all assumed the sender was the War Department, bearer of bad news.

In minutes neighbors would gather on your front porch, tap gently on the door and ask, "Is everything okay?" Very few homes or families were fortunate enough not to have someone off to war, so it built community in the neighborhood, a caring for one another.

There was no way Peggy would know whether I was dead or alive. But I had written her a letter one month earlier and said, "Peggy, if ever you are told that I'm missing or dead, don't believe it. I'm coming back!" I wondered if I had written that for my own benefit. I had to make it home. Peggy would be waiting.

It was early evening when we heard the first Jap search party. Different groups passed by most the evening. Their voices and movement kept us quiet in the pitch black. Twice we covered Lindley's mouth to silence moans. Otherwise, we barely breathed. The mosquitoes were eating us alive. The mosquito head-nets were a farce. You would sweat while trying to suck enough of the humid air through the fine mesh, and

CLASS OF SERVICE	WESTERN	1201	SYMBOLS
This is a full-rate Telegram or Cable-gram unless its de-ferred character is in-dicated by a suitable symbol above or pre-ceding the address.	UNION		DL = Day Letter
			NL = Night Letter
			LC = Deferred Cable
	A. N. WILLIAMS PRESIDENT		NLT = Cable Night Letter
			Ship Radiogram

The filing time shown in the date line on telegrams and day letters is STANDARD TIME at point of origin. Time of receipt is STANDARD TIME at point of destination

TGQ 6   45   GOVT. WASHINGTON D. C.   JAN. 18   1029A

MRS. MARGARET M. DUFFY
    8132 SO. WOOD ST. CHGO.

THE SECRETARY OF WAR DESIRES ME TO EXPRESS HIS DEEP REGRET THAT
YOUR HUSBAND FIRST LIEUTENANT WILLIAM F. DUFFY HAS BEEN REPORTED
MISSING IN ACTION SINCE ELEVEN JANUARY IN INDIA BURMA AREA IF
FURTHER DETAILS OR OTHER INFORMATION ARE RECEIVED YOU WILL BE
PROMPTLY NOTIFIED

                DUNLOP ACTING THE ADJUTANT GENERAL

                        947A

THE COMPANY WILL APPRECIATE SUGGESTIONS FROM ITS PATRONS CONCERNING ITS SERVICE

Peggy Duffy received this telegram from the War
Department on January 18, 1945, seven days after
the *Postville Express* went down over Malaya.

you couldn't see in the night.

At midnight, Talib returned. He brought cold rice, which we devoured with our dirty hands. Saltzman and Lindley had no appetite, but we forced them to eat.

Talib reported, "Three hundred Japs are searching jungle! You must move, this place no longer safe. Do not wear boots, they leave white man tracks and make too much noise!"

Despite our fear of snakes and whatever lived on the jungle floor, we removed our boots and followed Talib, barefoot in the dark. I guided Lindley, Carl had Saltzman, and Humphrey guarded our rear. The black night hid our path, yet Talib moved like a jungle cat.

The journey was torture. When you weren't in the open, where you had sky and starlight, you couldn't see, so you grabbed the man in front of you. The trail would slant to one side, then take a sudden drop—or we would fail to follow a bend and leave the trail. Leaves and branches slapped and scratched our bodies as we tried to advance quietly. Tangled in vines, tripping on roots or stepping in holes, we lost our footing and fell often. Mud and rotted vegetation left us dirty and wet.

At 0130 we came to a small farmhouse set in a clearing. Talib argued with an elderly Indian, who refused to help. He told Talib there was a search party of one hundred Japanese in the vicinity and anyone helping the Americans would die. But he gave us water, and Talib led us back to the jungle trail.

Thirty minutes later we arrived at another clearing. At the other edge, fifty feet away, stood a *basha*. Cautiously our eyes and guns scanned the fringe as we crossed toward the hut. The walls were dried branches stuck in the ground and tied together to a frame of larger ones. The roof was dried grass, lying over more branches set at a pitch. The entrance was covered by pieces of burlap, sewn together and tied to the top.

Talib led us into the dark *basha*, took a match and lit a wick that was sticking through a hole in the lid on a jar of kerosene. He placed it on a knee-high bamboo table. As the lamp cast light over the table, it revealed a horde of roaches and insects scurrying from the light. Tin bowls, cups, a pot covered by a filthy rag, scraps of food and the like remained.

The air carried a foul odor and chill from the dampness. Talib poked an old woman, who was sleeping on the floor in a corner, and told her to get some food.

Sitting on grass mats on the mud floor, we ate cold rice with our hands. I used one hand to fend off bugs and insects crawling up my legs from the floor.

Outside, a call startled us. Talib raised his hand to calm our fear. He pulled aside the burlap, revealing a Chinese man wearing shorts and a light-colored shirt, followed by a pretty Chinese girl with black shoulder length hair and dark eyes. She wore a pair of men's trousers, the legs rolled up several times, a hemp belt and a sleeveless pullover shirt. Both had olive to brown skin, with thin muscular bodies. They traveled barefoot. These people seemed to have leather feet, traveling the jungle trails unharmed while we nursed cuts, scratches and bruises on our feet and ankles.

Talib and the newcomers bowed to each other, then turned to us. It was quite a sight, everyone bowing in the small, one-room hut, close enough to butt heads. Talib introduced the man, "Wong Kwang," and the woman, "Liew Siew Yeng." They would be our guides from here.

Talib bid us farewell. "I must return home. I am sure that you will return home also. I am your very good friend. Please, if the Japanese catch you do not tell them my name. Do not tell them I helped you. Please, I am your very good friend!" Talib pledged.

"Talib, you have been extremely kind. Thank you for helping us. We will never forget you!" Hump said.

Each man shook hands with our Malay friend, expressed gratitude and bowed one more time before Talib vanished in the night.

Promptly, the young woman motioned us to leave. Outside she hoisted a large bundle of clothes on top of her head. How she managed was beyond me. The man carried a torch illuminating the trail around him and we maneuvered our way in the blackness.

"Just when we're starting to feel comfortable with Talib, he leaves!" Humphrey whispered. "Hell, these two don't even speak English!"

"All we can do is follow them," Saltz said. "We ought to call him 'George,' after the automatic pilot on our plane. We can call the girl 'Georgette!'"

We walked until daybreak. George led us to what appeared to be a deserted plantation. Silently, we skirted the plantation and climbed a small hill. George motioned us to sit, and said, "Muka . . . Muka," as he mimed eating. Humphrey nodded yes and George headed down the trail.

Cuts and scratches over our bodies were visible in the morning light, but our feet suffered most from the rough march. Exhausted, we collapsed on the jungle floor.

Talib Bin Ali & Samsudin Bin Sidek

Georgette & George
(Liew Siew Yeng & Wong Kwang)

Despite the pain stabbing my chest, Lindley and Saltzman's moans reminded me how fortunate I was. The burns were swollen, blistered and raw, and all we had was aspirin. As long as we were on the move, the morphine would have to wait. Georgette tore a piece of cloth from her bundle of clothes and used water from Lindley's canteen to clean the wounds. She picked off the dead skin, coated the burns in ointment and wrapped them with fresh gauze. Carl and I assisted, while Hump studied his map.

George returned with dried rice and sweet potatoes. We ate eagerly. The rice was hard to swallow, and even though the potato was uncooked, the sweet taste satisfied my stomach. Lindley's lips, blistered and swollen, hurt as he chewed and kept him from eating. Georgette fed Saltz, whose hands were giving him hell. Afterward, Lindley and Saltz fell asleep.

George put on quite a display for Hump, Carl and me. He pulled from his pocket Japanese money, spit on it and scowled. Squatting, he wiped his bottom with the paper, crumbled it, tossed it aside and smiled.

Standing, he took a small book from his pocket. The cover held a picture of Russia's Kremlin and a red flag with three golden stars in its upper corner. George pointed to each of the stars and rattled off the three major peoples of Malaya: "Chinese, Malay, Indian." At attention, he saluted us using a closed fist and outstretched arm, and yelled ecstatically in Chinese. Squatting before us, he smiled and said, "Me Communee! Me Communee!"

Georgette rose, saluted with fist and arm and cried, "Me Communee! Me Communee!" Next, she squatted beside George, picked up a twig, and etched seven stick figures in the dirt at our feet. The last five were shorter, maybe children. Chinese chatter detailing her story joined each action.

Pointing the twig at each child, she slashed its neck, decapitating all five children. Targeting one of the adults, she slit off hands and arms aimed at the head and sounded a small explosion. On the last figure she severed arms, legs and head.

Georgette scratched another person in the dirt, spread-eagle and bound by the wrists and ankles. She poked the twig at the figure and etched another body on top of it, an attacker. Counting the fingers of each hand, she stopped at nine and touched the picture with the twig. A moment passed and she smoothed the dirt. The picture vanished, but not the nightmare.

"Japs?" Humphrey asked, pointing where the picture had been.

Georgette nodded, "Yes!"

"Is she telling us her family was murdered and she was raped?" Carl asked.

"I don't know. I'm not even sure I want to know. She can't be more than 18!" I added. "The Japs have no moral decency. They're animals, murderers!"

George pointed to the trail. Approaching were a Chinese man and young Malay boy carrying a pot of hot tea and cups. Oh, what a welcome sight. The chill of the night still lingered in our muscles and bones.

The jungle has twelve hours of daylight, each day, every day. Shortly after six o'clock in the evening, darkness settles in and the temperature drops in this damp world. The jungle is always wet. The canopy of trees covering the floor seldom permits sunlight to penetrate and dry anything. Dreadful, hot and humid during the day and bone chilling at night.

The tea's warmth soothed the pain in my chest, relaxing me for the first time in twenty-four hours. Hump and I tended to Lindley and Saltz. The warm tea comforted them.

Georgette introduced our tea bearer, Lee Lok, and the boy, Karim. I was amazed that these people were eager to help despite the punishment of death if the Japs found out. Lee Lok sent Karim down the trail to stand guard and poured more tea while we relaxed against the jungle packs.

I closed my eyes and listened to the morning clamor of creatures. The sounds filled the jungle. Screams, barks, and chatter kept me from settling into sleep.

George jumped to his feet and looked down the trail at Karim, who was waving his arms over his head. Panic showed on the boy's face. He ditched into the thick growth along the trail. George screamed, clapped his hands and pointed down the trail.

"Lindley, Saltz, get up quick! Someone is coming," Carl said. He jerked Lindley to his feet, and I grabbed Saltzman.

"Duff, my burns, stop, you're hurting me!" Saltz cried.

"Quick, grab the gear and get the hell out of here!" Hump ordered.

"Japs!" I hollered. Thirty yards down the trail a patrol appeared. Three soldiers carried rifles with bayonets. How many more you couldn't tell, with the dense foliage.

Startled, they took cover along the trail and hollered in Japanese. I was damn scared! I didn't know whether they were calling to more Jap troops, readying to launch grenades, or open fire. As I reached for my pack and heaved it on my shoulder, I saw Lee Lok crawl into the brush and disappear.

The commotion prevented the Jap patrol from advancing, unsure of how many of us there were. The jungle trail seldom allows you to see much and you can't know how many men back up the ones you see, so you use caution.

George high-stepped into the jungle with Georgette's bare feet close behind. She lifted her bundle of clothes on top of her head, but dropped it a few feet later when the heavy vegetation tangled and tripped her. Free of the load, Georgette raced like a deer through the foliage.

Carl and I followed, wrestling with vines and bushes as they snagged our jungle packs and us. The heat and humidity robbed my oxygen and strength, but I wouldn't slow.

Humphrey, with those long legs, passed Carl and me and said, "We need to keep George in sight. We can't lose him!"

We ran for another fifteen minutes. Humphrey finally caught George by his shoulder and forced him to stop. All of us leaned over with our hands on our knees, catching our breath and dripping in sweat. While we did, Saltz caught up to us and plopped to the ground.

"Where's Lindley?" I asked.

"He ran the other way! I followed him till I saw you guys weren't behind us," Saltz said. "I called to him and said we were going the wrong way. He turned to look at me and ran into a tree. He laid there holding his leg and said, 'Go Saltz, get out of here, I think my leg is broke.' I said, 'Let me help you.' He yelled, 'Get the hell out of here, I'll go it alone!'

"So I ran back to the clearing and there was a Jap soldier clutching his rifle, twenty feet from me. I stopped dead, and so did he, and we stared at each other. I looked at his eyes. They were jumpy, moving from side to side. He was scared like me. I thought, 'He's going to shoot me as soon as his courage comes back and I will die.' So I made a break for it. I dove headfirst into the bushes and crawled on my hands and knees before the Jap acted. I tore through the growth!" Dirty, torn gauze dangled from his hands. Saltz held his hands waist high, fighting the pain. "Before I got to my feet, the Jap fired into the brush and scared the hell out of me. I expected to be shot. Two more rounds were fired as I took off on foot. I was so scared I couldn't think and I kept falling down. Luckily, the Jap didn't follow me into the brush, because he would have had me!"

"Probably waiting for his buddies rather than going in alone," Humphrey said. "It won't be long before they're here!"

"Lindley won't have a chance," I said. "His burns were giving him a bad time. He can't make it alone!"

"He has to. If we circled back now we would be in the Japs' hands. He's on his own and we need to move out!"

Everyone was silent as we caught our breath and thought of Lindley. If only he had run the other way. Out of eleven men, we were down to four. My nerves were on edge and my body was giving out. No sleep, little food, hundreds of Japs looking for us and now they knew where we were. I looked at each man—their faces showed their feelings. This was the nightmare we agonized over time and again before a mission, and now it was reality. What would become of our friends?

Georgette was in tears, I believe because she lost her clothes and possessions. This girl had had her share of hell on earth, enough for a lifetime. For three years her people had endured this lifestyle: uprooted from their homes and living in the jungle. Their parents, sisters and brothers, grandparents, friends, and neighbors murdered. Everything lost, only memories of life before the Japs invaded Malaya.

I felt guilty for my own sadness. Here stood Georgette, a young woman who should be dreaming of the possibilities of school, marriage, children, or just happiness. Instead she was fighting to stay alive and hold onto the bit of clothes and keepsakes left. I offered my handkerchief. She worked a brief smile, but refused the cloth I had used for the cut ring finger the day before.

In a few minutes we were back on our feet, continuing our flight from the Japs.

Georgette, leading, ran us another ten minutes. We crossed a clearing, jumped into a ravine and followed its course. Five minutes later, she led us out of the ravine and up a short hill. At the top, our

Chinese friends signaled us to crawl into the thick underbrush and demonstrated how we must bury ourselves beneath the rotting vegetation, using machete and hands.

Hump and Carl dug a bed for Saltz and covered his body from head to foot, leaving his face bare, while I buried the three jungle kits we escaped with.

Turning over the wet rot, we exposed centipede, spider, beetle, worm, every insect imaginable, living in this black decay. But it was our only choice, and we hurried to hide under the jungle humus.

The stench was disgusting and repulsive. My stomach climbed into my throat as I breathed in its nauseating foulness. Gagging, I was first to vomit.

A swarm of pests crawled on my body, entered my clothing and began dining on my flesh. I fought to remain still as I was bitten, but decided my gun hand would also serve to squish the pests between my flight suit and skin. They bit my face, neck, chest, arms, legs and privates. I had never known such torture, but I feared the Jap pursuit more.

Within thirty minutes, the voices and rustling of a Jap patrol drew near. The hacking of machetes grew louder. Their voices seemed closer. I cocked my pistol, then heard Hump and Carl do the same. George, lying beside me, raised his hands and pulled the pin on his grenade. He turned to me and smiled. I faked a smile back. This was too much.

Georgette clenched her machete. Somehow I doubted Georgette would surrender to the bastards. More likely, one or more would feel the cold, sharp steel of her machete enter his stomach before he died.

The Japs would have to kill her to stop her.

The enemy arrived. Machetes ripped through the brush leading to our hiding place. The chopping and hacking of grass surrounded our hilltop. I braced for the fight and prayed, "Heavenly Father, protect us, keep us in your embrace and lead us to safety."

The chopping seem to last forever, but gradually continued past us and could be heard over the next hour, along with the chatter of the Japs' voices. George replaced the pin in his grenade, and I carefully released the hammer on my pistol and returned it to its seat.

For nine hours we lay there afraid to make a brake, until the beat of a distant drum signaled the Jap troops to halt the search due to nightfall.

A half hour later, George instructed us to remain still while he slipped out and scouted. He returned with dried rice and a Chinese man who spoke broken English. He reported, "You are safe! Chinese friends will signal if the enemy return."

Lindley was captured. The man saw him led away by soldiers. His leg appeared injured, but not broken. His hands were tied. They whipped and beat his burned body and forced him to walk under his own power. The Japs showed no mercy.

We stared at one another. What could we say to make the situation better, more bearable? Lindley was in the hands of the enemy with his fate unknown.

We looked like hell and smelled worse. The rotting ground was saturated, and soaked its stench into our clothes and covered us in mud. The insect attacks created red welts and swelling, and the itching made us scratch the skin raw. The sun had set and we shivered in the evening's chill.

The day was a blur—it left me in shock or denial, nothing seemed real. Fighting for our lives and hundreds of Japs out to get us. Seven men missing, captured, or dead. Food, water and shelter questionable, along with our fate. Too much in this short time span. I wanted to wake up from this nightmare.

At 1830 we took to the trails. Total darkness slowed us and irritated George. Tired, dirty, wet, cold and hungry, we groped along. We endured endless mosquito attacks and, barefoot, we suffered more injuries and were slowed even more in our escape.

In less than forty-eight hours, we could barely continue. The Army Air Corps worked to keep its men in good physical condition, but climate in Southeast Asia is beyond anything we have in the States. Three degrees off the equator meant heat and humidity so high that when you swipe your hand through the air it comes back wet. Every inch of you and the jungle is wet. Breathing is labor, like a heavy person sitting on your chest. The struggle for oxygen tires you, blurring your mind.

At midnight we reached a railroad track with a road running parallel to it. Lying at the edge of the jungle, we watched a Malay guard leave a small building, walk around back and enter a latrine. As the man exited, George greeted him with a machete pressed to his throat and spoke to him. Then George released the guard, who hurried back to his post and closed the door.

He signaled by waving his machete and Georgette led us forward. We crossed the railroad track single file and squatted in knee-high grass in the shallow ravine between the track and the road, waiting for our next move.

Carl was first to hear it. He called, "Hit the dirt. A train is coming!" Landing on my stomach aggravated my chest injury, delivering a jutting pain and hampering my breathing.

"If that train begins to stop we hightail across the road and into the jungle," Hump said. "I'll give the call!" His rigid jaw and searching eyes revealed the tension he felt.

The train passed slowly, like a fast trot. Nine cars and an engine pushing northward. The train was loaded with Japs. The light from the rail cars illuminated their faces. They seemed to be staring down on us as we lay in the short grass.

Japs sat on the roof of each car with rifles, or manned a machine gun ready to cut us to pieces. There were a few hundred of them.

I forgot my chest pain. Instead, I could feel my heart pound. A cold sweat brought a chill and my hands perspired against the steel of the handgun.

Little damage could we inflict with our weapons, except the grenade clutched in George's right hand. I was beginning to like George's grenade.

After the train passed we got to our feet and headed up the ravine to the road. A vehicle appeared, casting headlights in our faces as it sped out of a curve.

We dropped to the ground and took aim with our guns. A jeep carrying six to eight Japs sped past, its lights revealing native sentries—Malay and Indian—posted every twenty yards along the road's edge. They would surely spot us if we tried to cross the road and escape into the deeper jungle.

With the jeep out of the way, George crawled silently along the road until he reached a sentry. In an instant, he had his machete on the man's throat.

Forcing the man to turn his back, he motioned us to cross the road, into the security of the dense jungle.

George mimed to the sentry how he would slash his throat—frightening him to keep silent—then he released the man and joined us in the brush.

The trip became more difficult. Hills covered with thick growth forced us to clear a path. We couldn't make ten minutes without resting. Sweat poured from us, and cramping muscles pleaded for water we didn't have.

Before daybreak we reached a farmhouse and ate boiled eggs and rice.

After sleeping a short time on a hill north of the town of Tampin, we continued the march until we came to a clearing where three Chinese guerrillas waited. Somehow, they knew George and Georgette were coming. The communication network among these people was proving vast.

We rested and slept while the Chinese kept guard. I woke to the smell of boiled duck—the whole duck—feet, head and all the innards, a Chinese delicacy. Our hunger won out, and we ate heartily.

There was a good-looking young man, clean and groomed, among the new Chinese. He wore a white shirt and dark shorts, and shoved food in his mouth so fast that Saltz named him "Commander Hog."

Another was skinny, short and dirty. A Jap bullet had crippled his right arm. We dubbed him "Nippon Joe."

The third man would come to be known as "The Spy." He was nervous, quiet, and followed the orders of the others.

I started a diary with scraps of paper I got from Commander Hog. I recounted our flight, the storm, the air battle, the wreck, the Japs, Lindley's capture, and our three days of trekking the jungle on little more than rice.

At 2330, Commander Hog took charge and started us walking. The brush grew thicker and the terrain had us climbing more hills.

Saltz was delirious and we had to guide him so he wouldn't wander off by himself. We walked through absolute darkness until the nine of us reached a clearing with two *bashas*.

Someone speaking very good English said, "Good evening, Americans! You are safe here. You are now at an outpost of the Second Guerrilla Regiment of the Malayan Peoples Anti-Japanese Army!"

The voice was that of a seventeen-year-old Chinese boy. He lit an oil lamp and smiled at us. "Please, come inside. You may sleep here!"

The lamp revealed a bed constructed of stakes in the ground with saplings stretched over them. Branches lay on top. They were covered with insects, crawling, nesting, or feeding.

Already there were eight Chinese men sleeping on the bed. Each one was as dirty as we were.

The boy woke the men and instructed them to

move over and make room for Hump, Carl, Saltz and me. Exhausted, we dropped to the twenty-foot-wide bed and passed out.

In the morning, there was a meeting with the outpost commander, who turned out to be our own Commander Hog.

The boy we had met in the early hours translated the conversation for Hog. The boy's name was Foo Lee Wong. He had learned English at a Methodist missionary school in Malacca, where they had baptized him Bartholomew. I liked his manners, smile and sincerity.

"I am very glad you have escaped the Japanese and have come to our camp!" Bartholomew translated.

"Thank you for your help, we are grateful," Hump answered.

Then Commander Hog broke into a lecture on how he despised the white man, particularly the British who promised to be back to help the Malayan people against the Japanese.

"We pleaded with the British to leave weapons, but the British stashed their supplies in the jungle and we had little luck locating them!" Hog spoke with venom.

"Thousands of Malay people are tortured and killed, but still the English did not return. Thousands of Communist ready to fight the Japanese, but need weapons. The United States also fails to supply our people weapons!"

The lecture continued for more than an hour. He did not wish to discuss any matters concerning our fate. He was intense in his distaste for the British and white men.

The remainder of the day, we were allowed to rest and sleep. We cleaned Saltz's hands and dressed the burns in fresh bandages. He was showing progress, but his condition was far from good.

Bites, cuts and bruises from our three-day journey plagued Hump, Carl and me. Infection became a problem as sores and cuts filled with pus and became painfully irritated and swollen, making it necessary for us to cut into the wounds and squeeze the matter from them.

With the extreme humidity, sores seemed to stay open forever. The climate's continual moisture seldom allowed anything to dry out.

So bruised and swollen were our feet that the Communists' insistence on our remaining barefoot to avoid leaving "white man tracks" wasn't hard to agree to.

We took to the trail at 1630, with Commander Hog, Nippon Joe, The Spy, George, Georgette, Bartholomew and two rifle bearers. Bartholomew told us, "We are traveling to a camp deeper in the jungle. It is reported that one thousand enemy troops are searching for you and a bounty of sixty thousand Japanese dollars is offered for your capture."

"Boy, they want us bad!" Carl said.

"Makes you wonder how many friends we have," I answered.

We walked until midnight. You couldn't see where you were going from one minute to the next. Saltzman walked off the trail and dropped twenty feet into a ravine, injuring his burned hands and cutting his forehead. We patched him up and took turns guiding him along the trail.

January 16, 1945—Rested till 0600 on a damp and cold terrace of an abandoned rubber estate, I recorded in my diary. Each night muggy air, bugs and insects prevented sleep, and damp clothing chilled us from head to foot. Another two-hour march and we stopped to eat rice.

"Cold rice," I groaned.

"I'll take yours, Duff," Carl joked.

"No thanks!" I laughed. This ignited my chest pain and tightened my breathing. Coughing added a tearing sensation. I lay back, closed my eyes, and the pain lessened.

"Duff, you okay?" Carl asked.

"It's my chest. The injury from the jump. I think it's a rib," I whispered. "I'll be okay. It seems to be better today."

"Open your flight suit, Duff, let's get a look."

I didn't argue. I unzipped the suit. Carl raised my T-shirt and cringed. From the collarbone to below the rib cage, my left side was a deep black and blue, mixed with blood clotting at the surface.

"Duff, this looks terrible! Hump, get a look at Duff's chest, he's got a bad bruise. He may be bleeding internally."

"Duff, you passing any blood?" Hump asked.

"First two days, but it quit. I'm sure it's the ribs, Hump."

"How about breathing. Talking seems to put a strain on you. Think you punctured a lung?"

"There's pain when I breathe, but it's the up and down movement of my rib cage. I don't think it's a lung."

"Can you go on?" Carl asked.

"Sure, climbing is tough, but maybe you could carry me, Carl!"

"Your jungle pack too," he said, giving me a light slap on the face.

At 1000 we continued. The trail led us into a swamp, first ankle deep and then waist deep. The smell was repulsive and each step sank into the muck bottom, making progress slow and difficult. Snakes and spiders were everywhere. Mosquito swarms made us crazy. There was no escape—they gorged on our blood, attacking by the hundreds.

Bartholomew came to our rescue. "Use the swamp mud to cover your face and neck. This will be a barrier to the mosquito."

Damned if it didn't work—at least, enough so that we could tolerate them.

Two miles into the swamp, Georgette let out a hair-raising scream that shook the jungle. She yanked at her legs, trying to remove jungle leeches sucking her blood. The Chinese men stood laughing at her, lending no assistance. I noticed giant leeches on me. Raising the right pant leg, I exposed six on that leg alone.

"Damn, look at these bastards! They're huge!" I pulled at a leech gorged with blood. "Look at the hole in my leg!"

Blood oozed from each spot the leeches had occupied. Most holes were the size of a quarter. The leeches had found their way to our legs, back, chest, and privates.

Humphrey and Carl joined in the search for leeches, exposing a number of them, as did the Chinese.

We removed Saltz's. He was delirious, running a fever and unable to comprehend the situation.

In the swamp, we kept a close watch. This came to be one of our most feared encounters of jungle life. The hole left by the leech would, without fail, become infected. They would scab, burst open releasing pus and blood, then cover over again. Weeks passed before they healed. In the end, these running sores left a sunken scar, usually about two inches long, but sometimes up to six inches.

It turned out that any time there was water, the giant leech was there. It was common to brush against foliage and pick up a waiting leech without knowing it, and be loaded down with eight to ten in no time.

Later that day, we came upon an open area where Japs had slaughtered an entire Chinese village—men, women, boys, girls, old, young—then used their scorched earth policy, setting fire to everything, including the bodies.

Bartholomew shared the story in tears.

"The Japs execute for fun! They hate Chinese, because we fight, we don't quit.

"Death comes from a firing squad or they blow your brains out with a pistol. But Japs like the slow death best. Stabbing with a bayonet, slicing off fingers, hands, and feet. Then chop an arm or leg off, finally the head!

"They light people on fire and laugh at the victim rolling in the dirt trying to put out the flames. Worse is their game of tossing a baby in the air and catching it on a bayonet, while the mother pleads. If the baby lives, they throw it again. Then, the mother is killed!

"Every time, they rape the women! Young, old, it does not matter to the Japs. They rape a girl and force her father and brother to watch, as each soldier takes a turn. They even force a father to rape his daughter and a brother to rape his sister or mother.

"They spare no one! The Jap says, 'This is a lesson for villages who hide or give food to the guerrillas.' The cruelty is typical. They are savages!"

Breathing through my blood-stained handkerchief cut the stench as I walked among charred bodies. Too many were children. If you could identify a corpse as a woman or young girl, it was always naked.

Swarms of flies and maggots created cavities in the slaughtered remains. Body pieces—arm, leg, hand, foot, head—lay throughout the village.

Back in India, we had heard stories of Jap atrocities, but I wasn't prepared for this massacre. "How could they do this?" I whispered. No one answered.

Seven days and thirty miles into the jungle, our party arrived at another Communist outpost. A large, curly-haired man, who shook hands and bowed continually, greeted us. Bartholomew translated his words.

"Welcome Americans! Happy and great pleasure to be in your company. You will stay here. There will be guards which will arrive and lead you in maybe a day," he reported, shaking hands again.

Saltz stepped back and raised his bandaged hands high to avoid any touch.

"Let's call him 'Joe Hollywood'—he reminds me of a press agent!" Saltz decided.

We washed out our clothes and bathed in a stream.

It brought life back to my filthy body. Without soap, I couldn't get my skin clean in the cool water. I didn't care. Just to rinse my clothes and be able to feel water against my skin was a delight. My normally thick black hair was matted with dirt and grease. I had to be content with just being able to comb through it. I came to appreciate each opportunity to bathe, regardless of the color of the water.

After a dinner of hot rice and eggs, Hollywood told this story.

"I was born in Jamaica and brought to Malaya when I was a child. My father was Chinese and my mother was American. Today, I am happy to be Communist. This is my duty to my brothers, Chinese and Malay. We unite to fight the British oppression of our people, which has been cruel for many years. They will return once the Japanese are defeated and we will fight them. This we do for our fatherland!"

"What have the British done to your people?" Hump asked.

"They own all the wealth, all the land and all the business! We are their coolies. We slave as rubber-tree tappers for seven or eight Strait dollars a month and rice to feed our family. It is against the law for a Malay or Chinese to farm land or take gold from streams. If we are caught they put us in jail, for we have broken their law!

"The British brought my people from China to provide cheap labor, for the Chinese are hard workers. The Malays are lazy and carefree! My people are brave and wish to have a better life. Because of this we are treated poorly.

"Malay children have free schools, but the Chinese have nothing. Without education we remain coolies to the filthy British!" Hollywood spit in disgust.

"Who will lead this fight against the British? Who will unite your people?" Carl asked.

"We have many friends! First we have been told of a great and powerful country that also fought as we must fight. They too did not have a good life. They wish to see us free—Chinese, Malay, and Indian—that we too may farm land and be educated. This very good country is Soviet Russia!

"The Malays show no interest, but the Chinese want a better life and the Communists will lead the way. We have leaders who left Malaya for years and returned much better leaders. We have thousands of Communist guerrillas throughout Malaya.

"Our leader is well educated and has been with us since the early 1930s. I have never met him and do not know his name—only the highest officers are allowed to be with him. It is known and accepted that he is a native of French Indochina.

"When the Japanese came in 1941 we were so happy. The British ran and we were free of their imperialism and oppression after many years. The Japanese promised each man a tract of land and distributed the possessions of the retreating British to the people.

"But over time the Japanese changed, they became brutal! They hunted our Communist leaders and executed many of our people. We retreated to the jungle to organize ourselves and carry on our fight for freedom. We changed our name from the Communist

Party of Malaya to the Malayan Peoples Anti-Jap Army. We did this so our people who hate the Japanese would join our fight.

"I am the Propaganda Officer for the Second Guerrilla Regiment. We have secret radios in the jungle, which give us news about Malaya and the rest of the world. We print this news and tell all the good that the Anti-Jap Army is doing for our people. We make thousands of copies of our newspapers, the *Voice of Liberty*, *Victory Herald*, and the *Voice of Malaya*, so all can know in Malaya this wonderful thing we do."

"Hump, radios! Tell him we need to get to head-quarters," I said. "Maybe we can radio for a submarine!"

Hump nodded and said, "Bartholomew, ask if he will take us to this leader of yours. Tell him we need his help to get home!"

Hollywood's response was, "It is highly unlikely that you will ever get out of Malaya or be allowed to go to Communist headquarters, but you may write a letter to our supreme commander requesting permission for an interview."

That evening Humphrey wrote the letter to the supreme commander requesting an interview. Runners would carry the letter through the jungle. A response could take two weeks.

"Write a letter to the Malayan people asking them to take up arms against the Japs!" Hollywood added.

Polite, but firm, Hump said, "No, not at this time, but we will when we reach headquarters."

At breakfast the next morning we went through a discussion of who would possess our guns after we left the outpost. We refused to relinquish our guns, and

Hollywood had Bartholomew explain the Communist system in Malaya. Hollywood was commissioner in charge of the political setup in the Second Regiment and he "needed the guns"!

"As if we don't!" I said.

We agreed to sign a paper stating we would send the guns back to them, after completing our journey in Malaya. This could be indefinitely.

The fourth day a note arrived from higher headquarters. "The Americans are to be moved deeper in the jungle." George and Georgette would not be joining us. We each took our turn to bid farewell.

"Thank you! We will never forget you and your kindness," I said through Bartholomew. Our smile, handshake and bow were hardly a reward for risking their lives for our safety. Georgette said, "Happy are we to help you from the enemy. It brings great satisfaction to hurt the Jap murderers!"

Four hours and six miles of dark jungle later, our tired bodies came to the camp of Yung Han and a garrison of fifty men. A clearing, one hundred yards wide, served as a parade ground. Five *bashas* stood along the edge, hidden from aerial view beneath trees, each sleeping ten men.

Every morning at six, rain or shine, Yung Han drilled his men up and down the parade ground. But marching and drilling in English style had no value in a jungle war.

Most Communists had rifles left behind by fleeing British, but few had more than ten cartridges. The penalty for losing a cartridge was to stand in the sun aiming a rifle for a couple of hours. If a man collapsed, he was revived and brought to his feet to continue the punishment.

The troops were skin and bone, clothed in anything from a loincloth to an old, frayed European suit. Shoes were handmade of solid rubber, weighed a ton, and made your feet hot and sore. Most chose barefoot, especially when journeying through the jungle.

"There will be a party in your honor tonight!" Bartholomew interpreted for Yung Han.

After a dinner of fish balls and sugar cake, Yung Han led us into the largest *basha*, a gathering hall for lecture and celebration. Yung Han's entrance lifted thirty men to their feet, who gave their leader a clenched-fist salute.

Joining the Chinese on narrow, makeshift benches, we faced a stage where Yung Han spoke a moment and then the entire group shot to their feet and sang a military marching song in Chinese.

Bartholomew wasn't present to translate the five Chinese who took turns giving talks. The Communists smiled and nodded to us throughout the speeches. They knew of the B-29 bomber, the only phase of the Allied effort helping Malaya, and we happened to be part of a B-29 crew. This served us well.

After another song, we were coaxed to the stage to sing. We sang "I've Been Working on the Railroad" and "You are My Sunshine." We were a hit. The applause and cheers urged an encore, so we came back with "Down by the Old Mill Stream" and "Jingle Bells." We weren't good, but the Chinese thought we were great.

From his camp, Hollywood sent some wine and boric acid, used as a weak antiseptic, as a present to us.

We invited Yung Han and some of his boys to the *basha* we shared for a drink. The wine was terrible, but the fresh eggs that Yung Han provided were delicious.

"Bartholomew, where did the eggs come from?" Saltz asked.

"Each camp has one or two farms operated by our people who are too old to fight. Some farmers who are not Communists also give us food, clothing, money and weapons. If they don't, that brings them suffering or maybe death."

The following day other gifts were presented. Coffee, sugar, milk and a book by H.G. Wells, *In the Days of the Comet*. We had no idea who sent it, but apparently there were plenty of farmers sympathetic to the Allies' cause.

Yung Han gave us a sliver of soap, which lasted three days. It was six weeks before we would see soap again. We also received a toothbrush made of bone and wild boar bristles stitched together. All four of us shared the toothbrush until it fell apart.

On January 27, The Spy was brought into camp as a prisoner. The next day there was a court-martial, during which he was given a chance to show his true colors. He was accused of betraying the Communist guerrillas in a meeting with the Japs and was found guilty, so the Communists executed justice.

All the guerrillas were present, as were the four of us. His hands were bound with cord behind his back. They fitted cord around his neck and led him to a large tree at the edge of the camp clearing.

The end of the cord was thrown over a thick branch and wrapped behind the trunk of another tree.

They pulled until the heels of his feet barely touched ground, and tied it off.

His eyes bulged and his face turned red, as he gasped for air. There was chatter and laughter among the guerrillas, but Hump, Carl, Saltz and I were silent. It was disturbing how these men saw humor in another man's misfortune.

After nearly ten minutes, Yung Han gave an order and two guerrillas came forward. Each had a rifle with bayonet. They taunted The Spy with fake thrusts of the bayonet, laughing as he cringed in anticipation of the piercing blade.

Finally, a blade pierced The Spy's left thigh and the guerrilla twisted the bayonet in the muscle as he withdrew it. Blood flowed from the puncture, down his leg and over his foot.

The Spy collapsed and choked, with the noose tightened around his neck. Despite the hole in his thigh, he rose to his feet—the cord having stretched from his collapse—which allowed him to breathe. Beads of perspiration formed on his face and he struggled to stand.

Yung Han allowed him to suffer a few minutes, and then gave an order for the other guerrilla to repeat the act on The Spy's right thigh.

Again he collapsed, hanging by the noose, as blood ran from the torn flesh, down his thigh and fell to the ground.

The guerrilla talk and laughter grew louder. His suffering excited them. The noose cut into his neck and he couldn't breathe. He planted one foot, then the other, and stood. The noose did not slacken and again he collapsed.

His face turned deep blue and purple, and he bit through his tongue. The pain proved too much and he lost consciousness.

His body quivered, his face bulged, and blood ran from his nose and seeped from behind his eyes, down his cheek. His bladder gave way and he wet his pants.

Unconscious, The Spy died before the bayonet pierced his heart and blood flowed from the gash in his chest.

The guerrillas' amusement and joy with the execution troubled me deeply. Their laughing, joking, and the satisfaction they seemed to get through the cruel death of their enemy.

Three years of jungle life and death to family and friends fed their hunger for revenge, but I couldn't help thinking of them as sharing the worst habits of the Japs.

The following morning we received a dinner invitation. "Good morning, Lowe-Shin," Hump said. We named him "English Tom." He was an interpreter for Yung Han, who murdered English translations.

"You are guest to banquet."

"In camp, English Tom?" Hump asked.

"No, we journey *kampong*."

About noon, English Tom and ten guards led us on a five-hour walk. Reaching Tom's home, near Dangi, we rested an hour. In the last mile, we came to the main road between Tampin and Kuala Pilah. The sign at our crossing read T-23. There were now one thousand Japanese at Tampin.

"Is this a good idea, Tom?" Carl asked. "Are we safe

with the Japs so close?"

"Not worry!"

"He's either very brave or very stupid," I whispered to Hump.

"I bet stupid, Duff!"

The road was empty and we crossed in pairs, while guards watched both directions. With the road behind us and secure in the jungle cover, we pushed on.

In minutes our path led to a rocky ledge high above a river. We crossed on a log, one hundred feet long and fifty feet above the water. Below, rocks and branches lined the narrow river as its current swept through lush greenery. Barefoot, I could grip the log with my toes for balance, but when I looked down my confidence fell. It took some time for each of us to balance our way to the opposite side, but we all managed without incident.

"What a hair raiser," I said to Carl, arriving on the other side. "This is crazy!"

"Yeah, this isn't my idea of fun. I'm losing interest in Tom's banquet quite fast."

At 1730, we arrived at a cluster of *bashas* in a little clearing. The Communists posted guards at every trail leading into this *kampong*, or village, because within a few miles was a village occupied by Japs.

Directed to a yard near a *basha*, we found three chairs waiting for the four of us, their "guests of honor." We took turns sitting, while people filed by to shake our hands and greet us with smiles.

Close to fifty Malay and Indian attended. Most wore festive linen, wrapped around their bodies and tucked shut, known as a sarong. But I was most intrigued by the women and children's faces painted with rice powder. English Tom said, "You Americans come to free Malaya, the people honor you and celebrate."

During the greeting, the cackle of chicken behind the *basha* announced part of the menu. It was our first genuine meal in three weeks.

We met Mohammed Pilus, the Malay who invited us to the banquet. He spoke five languages and told us, "The reason I invite you, is so you will remember me after war." I found this peculiar and thought, *We'll see!*

"You Americans made much damage at Singapore with bombs," Pilus smiled.

"What did you hear?" Hump pressed.

"Destroyed was landing dock for Japanese Navy and ship."

"Ship, what kind of ship?" Hump said.

"One with big guns and fast."

"A cruiser?"

"I am thinking it was cruiser."

We slapped one another on the back in celebration. Mission accomplished. The *Postville Express* wasn't lost without a price to the Japs, if Pilus had his information correct.

"We have word of other Americans with you!" Pilus said. "Three men die, two in hospital, and two in prison in Kuala Pilah." This killed our jubilee. We were stricken by this news.

After some description and questions, we figured that Marty Govednik and an enlisted man about twenty-nine years old, possibly left gunner Gillett, were in prison. It appeared that Spratt, Govednik, and Gillett had been hidden and cared for by a friendly Malay. Spratt, severely burned, begged his buddies to kill him. He suffered for thirty-six hours before he died. His body was left at the crash site and found one morning by our friend, Talib. After one week, the Malay—afraid of Jap reprisal—led the Japs to Govednik and Gillett.

Mick Kundrat's body was found in the plane. He always said, "If we go down, I'm not bailing out. I can't stand the thought of the Japs getting hold of me."

Colonel Billings was dead, buried chest deep in the rice paddy field near the main fuselage of our B-29.

The two in the hospital were most likely Ralph Lindley, with his burns, along with top gunner MacDonald.

I was numb with the news. Seven buddies captured or dead, just like that. I hated this war. I looked at Carl, who was staring at the ground before him. Saltz studied his hands and Hump looked at me without speaking. What could we say to this nightmare?

"Our people wish to know, why man with curly dark hair is tall and skinny and why two men have blue eyes, " Pilus inquired.

We looked at Hump and laughed.

"Tall, dark and handsome doesn't cut it here, Hump," Saltz teased. Hump had a boyish look for twenty-five. He was over six feet tall, with dark brown hair and brown eyes. Carl, though not quite six feet, had a large frame, sandy brown hair and blue eyes. Saltz stood about five seven with a light frame, brown hair and brown eyes. At five nine, I sported a solid build I acquired through boxing and athletics in high school, and had maintained in the military. And my eyes? Well, Peggy had always said, "You have beautiful, piercing blue eyes!"

I could understand the curiosity of these people. The Malay, Chinese, and Indian tend to have dark hair, dark eyes and similar skin color, for the most part. Along come four white men, and each is different.

English Tom interrupted Pilus and said, "The people request American news of war against Japan and Germany."

When Humphrey stood to address our admiring hosts, Saltz took his chair. English Tom was interpreter.

"Thank you for your kindness and friendship. The banquet was delicious!" Humphrey began. The rest of us smiled, nodded and patted our full stomachs.

"We are happy to say that the Allies are pounding away at the homelands of Japan and Germany. Every day they continue to bring them closer to their knees." This prompted cheers from our hosts. "The Americans and the B-29 bombers are destroying the Japanese in Malaya. They continue to lead the fight to free your people and country from the Japanese aggressors. They will not stop until Japan is defeated!"

Smiles in the crowd and the applause reflected the hatred they held within. The excitement showed hope for their future and Malaya. These kind and generous people wanted the suffering and bloodshed to end. They were delighted by Humphrey's report and carried on their discussion among themselves.

English Tom said to Humphrey, "We wish you to tell people how Anti-Jap Army care for you. How we put up great fight against Japanese and causing much trouble and defeat everywhere. That we are bringing freedom. That Anti-Japs will appreciate support. Food, money, clothes and weapons."

Humphrey ignored him and sat down in the chair I offered. English Tom scowled at Humphrey, but said nothing. We did not intend to be used by the Communists to delude these people.

The evening was rounded out by the four of us singing "The Army Air Corps Song," at the people's urging. We stood and faced the hosts:

Off we go into the wild blue yonder,
Climbing high into the sun;
Here they come zooming to meet our thunder,
At'em boys, give 'er the gun!
Down we dive spouting our flame from under, off
with one helluva roar!
We live in fame or go down in flame,
Nothing'll stop the Air Corps now. . . .

On our return we stopped off at an Anglo-Indian's and finished off a stalk of bananas with our tea. Actually, Saltz finished them. He shoved fifty-six bananas in his mouth before he called it quits. It was less than pretty with the belching and other bodily noises—if Saltz had social graces, he hid them well!

We caught sleep at English Tom's place until early dawn.

Halfway to camp, we heard tremendous explosions and later saw formations of fourteen B-29s high overhead, bombers operated by good friends in our outfit, the Twentieth Bomber Command, returning to India.

"Imagine they hit Singapore!" I whispered.

1st Lt. Marty Govednik; 1st Lt. Cliff Saltzman; Major
Don Humphrey; 1st Lt. Bill Duffy; T/Sgt. Mick Kundrat

T/Sgt. Dana Gillett; S/Sgt. John MacDonald;
T/Sgt. Ralph Lindley

"They look damn good!" Carl uttered. "Wish we were with them."

The Communist laughed, pointing at the four of us staring in disappointment at our airplanes. English Tom continued the ridicule and urged the others on until the planes were out of sight. We ignored the mockery. Instead, we dreamed of being with our friends . . . headed home.

B-29 Superfortress

1st Lt. William F. Duffy's dog tags

Jungle Fever

February 1 marked the beginning of "black water fever." It struck me, then Carl five days later. It began with a headache, weariness and nausea. In the evening I was hit with a terrible chill. I covered myself with a blanket, but my body shook and perspired as I burned with fever. My breathing was rapid and I drifted in and out of consciousness.

By the third day my symptoms had grown worse. My muscles cramped from lack of fluids. My buddies forced quinine, tea and water down me, fighting dehydration, but frequent vomiting reduced the effort. There was nothing beyond the quinine for medicine, other than aspirin, which was useless. They kept me covered and took turns wiping the sweat from my face and neck with a wet cloth.

In the early hours of the fourth day, the fever broke and my temperature dropped. Carl, who was tending me, escorted me to a path in the jungle, where I vomited and fell victim to diarrhea. Abdominal pain, cramps and increasing weakness continued and by evening the fever returned.

Carl became ill the following day. Nausea, head-ache, weakness, followed by fever and chills—my exact path. Humphrey and Saltzman worked on both of us with little success. I was worse with the second bout of fever. They say I became quite delirious and rambled on about Peggy and fought our last air battle over and over. Carl's illness appeared to be less severe.

Two days later, I put in the worst day of my life. At times I didn't think I would last through the day. Finally, in the evening, the fever started to break, and two hours later it was nearly gone. I slept most the night, the first time in six days.

Carl's rapid deterioration took him in and out of consciousness. Delirious, he too fought our last air battle over and over, screaming, moaning, crying out, then collapsing exhausted, weaker from each lapse of fever.

It appeared we suffered from malaria and cholera, or typhoid fever. Carl and I were losing between one and three gallons of fluid per day from diarrhea. The runny bowel movements were endless, sometimes ten to fifteen minutes apart. It wasn't long before we soiled our clothes and were forced to lie in them, while insects took interest.

Hump and Saltz fought to keep fluids in us. Dehydration meant death for Carl and me.

The *basha* was not much more than a roof. Flying

insects, spiders and crawling bugs met little resistance. The hard bed of stretched saplings and branches was home to them and the four of us. Without fail, we were continually awakened at night and each morning found new welts, bites, infections and swelling.

On the evening of February 8, the Communist guerrillas had another social. Carl and I—dizzy and weak—attended, but Carl had to leave early; he began to feel sick. The fever and chills were mounting again. I found myself singing a solo, "You Are My Sunshine," and later joined Hump and Saltz in singing "Six Pence." Before the social ended, I became ill and joined Carl in the *basha*.

Throughout the night the two of us suffered. Everything came back double. Vomiting many times, watery diarrhea, shaking with fever and little sleep. The next day was exactly like the night before.

After futile attempts to pressure Yung Han for help, Hump lost his temper. He demanded that Yung Han get a doctor or some medicine. Yung Han agreed to send a runner to a doctor in an Indian village. Hump wrote a note describing the illness and three days later the runner returned with stomach pills, which were of no help, and a note telling the Americans to come to him and he would give them medicine for their friends. Hump and Saltz thought it was a Jap trap, but decided to make the journey in hopes of helping Carl and me. In the meantime, Carl and I were getting worse.

The next afternoon a note from Humphrey arrived by runner:

Dear Duff and Carl,

*We met with the doctor and he believes you are
suffering from malaria and cholera. The quinine water
and cholera mixture accompanying our note should be
taken immediately.*

*We arrived at Lowe-Shins and received word from
Communist HQ. It instructs us to go to HQ to begin
arrangements to depart from Malaya. Saltz and I have
decided to proceed as instructed. We hope to see you as
soon as you are able to travel.*

Hump

"What about us!" I hollered. The runner delivering the note flinched. "How the hell are we supposed to make it out of here?" Carl stirred and I showed him Humphrey's note. "The bastards are gone, Carl!" Carl shook his head and lay back down, too weak to talk. The quinine water that Hump spoke of in his note was missing—only the cholera mixture remained.

"This is beautiful, just wonderful, the damn Communists took the quinine. Where's the quinine!" I yelled. The runner cringed and darted from the *basha*.

"Carl, how are you?"

"I'm drained, Duff. I have no strength."

"We have to fight this, Carl. We have to make it out of here!"

"I have doubts, Duff. We can't even get off this bed to relieve ourselves." He was right. Both of us were getting worse.

That day, a friend named Asui took it upon himself to send Humphrey a note, telling him to return, that Carl and I were worse. We told him no,

that a decision had been made and we were on our own.
I wrote in my diary, without knowing why.
What good is it to record your death? Still, it seemed
to matter.

*Feb. 13, 1945—Hell! That is the only word to
describe this day. Carl getting worse. I took the cholera
mixture, but Carl didn't. I started to feel a little better,
but about 1500 we almost lost Carl. I then had the
guerrillas force the liquid mixture down him and now
we are all praying for good results. He hasn't had control
of his mind since about noon. He seemed to work up to
a climax and then it seemed like he passed the crisis about
2000. I'm for a change in scenery & diet for the both of us.*

Nearly all night we worked on Carl. Medicine,
fluids, and damp rags to break his fever. His breathing
was heavy and there was a raspy noise in it.

Before dawn Carl stopped gasping and I crawled
alongside him. I couldn't feel Carl's heart beat, so I
grabbed his wrist, where I found a faint pulse. I
mounted him and began resuscitation. I collapsed
from my own weakness and landed on the *basha* floor.
The Chinese lifted me back on the bed beside Carl.
Then one man, understanding what I had attempted,
took over resuscitating for the next twenty minutes.

I lay beside Carl holding his wrist and praying.
Finally, he let out a gushing sound and vomited clots
of blood, like coffee grounds.

Moments later, I couldn't feel a pulse.

Carl was dead!

I lay with my friend's body, wishing this were a
nightmare. Carl and I had trained together for the Air

sent a letter trying to have them return here, seeing how bad Carl + I had gotten. Another letter arrived the next day, but apparently A - Sins' didn't reach him. They sent some Cholera mix and epsom salt in with the message.

Feb. 13, 1945

Hell! That is the only word to describe this day. Carl getting worse. I took the Cholera mixture! but Carl didn't. I started to feel a little better. but about 1500 we almost lost Carl. I then had the guerilla force the liquid mixture down him and now we are all praying for good results. He hasn't had control of his mind, since about noon. He seemed to work up to a climax and then it seemed like he passed the crisis about 2000. In for a change in scenery + diet for the both of—

Feb. 14, 1945

Carl passed away at 0535 this morning. We worked on him nearly all night, but unfortunately to no avail. I'm a nervous wreck and my condition is worse. I pray it comes before my number is also called. Wrote a letter to Don immediately telling him the sad news. Buried Carl at 1030 and I'm naming—

Duffy's diary entries February 13-14, 1945
detailing the death of his good friend Carl Hansman.

Corps, flown to India, carried out missions and fought the enemy.

Now, was I to die with him?

I was a nervous wreck and my condition was worse.

Weeping and grieving, I prayed aid would come before my number was also called. For the next five hours I lay looking at Carl. Insects and bugs grew in number on the corpse, nauseating me. I protected my friend from the invaders until he was carried away for burial. It was during this time I made up my mind that I would live. I was determined to make it home, to Peggy and our children.

"If I die, it will be during my journey in the jungle, not in this camp, not in this bed. I'll make it, Carl!"

I wrote a letter to Hump and Saltz, telling them the sad news.

February 14, 1945

Dear Don & Saltz:

I'm not sure of the date or anything right now, but I'll try to make this note understandable. Carl passed away this morning at 0535. They are going to bury him today. His condition had gradually gotten worse since you left and several times I thought he was gone, along with my own life. Well I can't give any details now, but that's the very sad picture.

The first day you left Asui sent a letter asking you to return. Naturally Carl & I didn't want you to, but apparently that letter never reached you. I pray this one does.

I think by the time you receive this I'll be ready to

travel. I would appreciate it, Don, if you would return and assist me with this luggage. The past days have been miserable, because nobody understands what you want or need.

Well, good luck fellows and let's hope we're together soon.

As always,

Duff

About 1030 the guerrillas came to the *basha* and removed Carl's wristwatch and identification tags. I made them put one tag back around his neck. They wanted to take his clothes, but I wouldn't permit them. I would not allow my friend to be buried naked. They wrapped the body in a grass mat, hoisted it on a pole and carried it from the *basha*. That was the last I saw of my good friend, Carl. They buried him in a shallow grave in the Malaya jungle.

Over the next five days I gained strength, while combating periods of fever and stomach pain. Three men—Loong Nam, Tie Shing, and Ah Na-tie—moved into the *basha* after they washed down the other side of the sapling bed. They fed, washed, and cared for me. My names for them were "My Boy," "Cookie," and "New Man."

It was February 19, 0600, that I awoke and was told the Japs were searching the jungle and the camp was on alert. Everyone was to be ready to leave on a moment's notice. I packed Carl's and my gear, along with the gear Humphrey and Saltzman had left behind. Carl's and my guns were missing.

"My Boy, where are the guns?" I pointed my finger, cocked my thumb and shot bullets from my mouth. My Boy shrugged his shoulders and shook his head side to side. I looked at Cookie and New Man, who gave the same answer.

During my illness I had attempted to keep the Communists out of our gear, but lost the guns. But they didn't take the shells, which amused me. All the rain ponchos were gone too. They knew the value of rain gear in a tropical rain forest.

At 1000 the boys who had escorted Hump and Saltz—Tommy Gun Lad, Running Guard and Straw Hat returned. Bartholomew was with them. They handed over a note to Yung Han from Humphrey, stating that he may be moving in three days to another camp. Yung Han passed the note to me.

"Yung Han, I need to leave camp today, now!"

"There is no way that you can travel safely. The Japs are searching the jungle for you."

"That's understood, it's my responsibility, my choice."

"I cannot allow you to travel today, perhaps tomorrow will be better."

"Yung Han, my friends are making plans to leave Malaya, they say they're moving to another camp, and it's three days' travel from here. I must reach them before they leave!"

"We must wait and see if the Jap troops give up their search."

I feared being left in Malaya and worried of my chance for survival, with such poor health. I continued pushing on Yung Han to permit my travel.

At 1300 he gave in, and we departed that day.

Chee-Fa-Pu

Asui, Tommy Gun Lad, Running Guard and Straw Hat were my escorts. We arrived at English Tom's place at 1430. I was worn, but persuaded them to move on that night. By sundown, however, I was in no condition to continue, so we spent the night. I questioned my ability to last the trip and prayed for strength.

At 0600, as we were leaving, a young lad arrived from camp flaunting my .45, so I swiped it back. "This is mine, son, and I need it!" Poking it into the holster, I shouldered it and positioned the gun under my left arm.

We began the day's eleven-hour journey, damp and cold from the night. Battling thick vegetation and vines with a machete was exhausting, and eventually I could barely hold the blade in my hand. Insects bit, while the leeches sucked until full and exposed the next hole for infection.

Brushing certain plants or bushes spread a rash or cuts over my skin, irritated by sweat and a delight to attacking insects. Sweat was endless, drenching my clothes all day and delivering a horrible chill by early evening.

Each day I would try to wash out my shorts and undershirt in a stream or river. It was impossible to keep up with the mud, sweat, rain and swamp. For days I would live in muddy wet clothes, until I stopped for a day. Most of the time, washed clothes would still be wet in the morning, but I wore them anyway. You learn to live with almost anything when you have no choice.

If a path was flooded or washed out by heavy rain, we pushed on, whether ankle or chest deep. I was always wet and covered in mud.

Delirious and weak, I staggered on. Often I collapsed on the trail, took the fetal position and shivered with fever. My thoughts drifted and I wasn't alert. I worried that I might be careless at a crucial time. Ten to fifteen minutes would pass and the guards would stop so I could catch up.

The stench of stagnant water and rot on the jungle floor nauseated me and I vomited, stealing strength and energy.

I prayed often and carried a little book written five hundred years ago by Thomas à Kempis, *The Imitation of Christ*. It reminded me of my dependence on God's love and the futility of life without it. I knew I couldn't survive on my own and asked God for strength.

I didn't want Peggy alone, raising our children. I hardly knew my son, Danny, seventeen months old. It was a year since I had seen him. And now I had a daughter, Peggy Anne, four months old. Fire-engine red hair like my lover and best friend.

These thoughts kept me in the fight and pushed me on. I had to make it back, I had promised Peggy, *"If they tell you I'm missing or dead, don't believe it, I'm coming back!"*

Midmorning, we reached the road to Tampin. Each man crawled to the edge, to survey the road. All clear, he would dash and plunge into the foliage on the other side.

Straw Hat and Tommy Gun Lad made it safely. Running Guard stood me up for my turn. I struggled to the road and paused. I stepped on the road, but was jerked to the ground and dragged back to the ditch by Running Guard.

Just then a lorry of Jap soldiers came by. Running Guard lay on top of me and covered my mouth, while the lorry passed and continued down the road.

"Thank you, Running Guard, thank you!" I shook his hand and bowed my head. A fleeting thought reminded me of the Jap promise: "To kill any survivor from a B-29 for their terror from the skies on the Japanese mainland!"

We climbed many hills and I fell again and again. Rain made it a slippery climb up slopes of mud and rotted leaves. The humid air hampered breathing and left me soaked in perspiration. The guards grew impatient with me, for the journey was taking twice the time it usually would.

We reached the Muar River. The Communist guerrillas had previously rigged a crossing, constructed of steel cable, stretching across the nearly sixty foot wide river.

There were two cables, one above the other. You gripped the top one with your hands, while you walked along the lower cable. Jap patrol boats policed the river, trying to cut off Communist supplies that were known to be carried up and down by boat.

I watched as Tommy Gun Lad, Running Guard, and Straw Hat made the crossing. Movement of the cable would cause them to swing back and forth, but this didn't seem to disturb my barefoot Chinese friends.

Asui and I were last to cross. With a jungle pack on my back, I took one step and upset the lower cable. My foot slipped and I hung clenching the upper cable in both hands, swinging back and forth at the river edge.

Catching the lower cable with my foot, I was able to stop swinging, then balance both feet on the cable. Resting, I looked at Asui, who smiled and shook his head.

I started slowly over the river—eighteen feet below—making my way to the other side. With the cable swinging back and forth, I gripped tightly and slid my feet along with care. I paused and stared as the swollen river tossed branches and debris in its current.

This was labor and my illness had sapped my strength. Shavings from the cable worked their way into my hands and feet, stinging and drawing blood.

Past the halfway point, I slipped. My hands were stripped from the upper cable. As I went down, I

caught the bottom cable behind my knees and swung
back and forth, upside down, like a monkey. The
Chinese were screaming from both sides of the river.
I didn't understand their words, but I knew it concerned me.

Gathering strength, I reached up to grab the foot
cable with one hand. I had it, but the weight of the
pack pulled me down. My next attempt failed too.

I tried to remove the pack, but it was too tightly
drawn to my body. I had nothing left. Blood raced to
my head and breathing was difficult hanging like this.

If I let go I would have the river's current to
contend with. I would have to shed the pack the
moment I hit the water, because its weight would pull
me under. I was a good swimmer, but not today!

As I hung there, Straw Hat on one side and Asui
on the other made their way out to me. The two
scrawny men each took an arm and pulled until they
had me sitting on the lower cable, then held me by the
straps of the pack until I could muster enough strength
to pull myself up by the upper cable.

I lay against the cable, exhausted. I couldn't lift
my head. Nauseated, I spewed bile to the river below.
Cramps gnawed at my stomach. My friends stayed at
my side, until I was finally able to reach the shore.

I collapsed on the bank. After a needed rest, we
moved on to a Malay's hut and slept the night. We
rested the next day until late afternoon—much to my
delight.

Pouring rain began again as we returned to the
jungle trail. The guerrillas knew of a *basha* atop a hill,
where we waited until the rain eased. Again, we set out,

crossing a railroad track and a road safely in the early evening.

Another downpour forced us into the shack of a small Eurasian man. He shared the mud floor home with his pigs. There was no sleep that night! The squeal, snort or scream of pigs shook my nerves. Foul dung raised my body hair and gagged me, and its odor penetrated my clothes. I wasn't sure the rain would be a poor choice over the pigs.

For another two days, the five of us continued our bout with water, mud, leeches, torrential downpour, insects, and dense jungle—always tired, wet, muddy and hungry.

Rice was the main staple each day, every day. Cooked, uncooked and always a potential threat to the digestive system not accustomed to jungle parasite, bacteria, fungus, virus or germ.

Food was possibly the worst enemy of the Communist guerrilla, carrying disease and illness from the unsanitary conditions in which it was prepared. Water came from river, pool or spring and into the pot. Of course, this was our drinking water. No choices, living in the jungle!

One day's journey from "Chee-Fa-Pu," I sent this note to Humphrey and Saltzman:

Feb. 23, 1945

Dear Don & Saltz:

I'm at an outpost about 10 hours from you and am leaving tonight as soon as English Tom arrives. See you tomorrow. The Chinese carrying this note are leaving now—0800—and I thought I'd explain the reason for our luggage arriving ahead of me. Feeling fine—Bill

English Tom arrived and we set out at 1600. It turned out that Yung Han's men were being moved to Chee-Fa-Pu. I wish they had decided this before I carried the luggage for five days.

My health, while improving, still slowed our progress. I was constantly watched, since I would wander aimlessly or plop down on the trail.

English Tom intended us to reach the camp that evening, but with my pace it could not be done.

As evening approached and shadows appeared, we entered Dunlop Estates, a rubber plantation. We moved quietly, using hand signals to communicate on the way. The chatter of jungle birds covered the sound of our steps as we passed buildings and the main house.

There were three roads to contend with. Two were within the plantation. The third ran from the farm to the intersection of the road that carried traffic between the towns of Bahau and Rompin.

It was at this road that I had just left the ditch to make my way to the other side, when a car approached at about ten miles an hour.

I was at the road's edge when the headlights cast their beam in my direction. My reflexes were dull and I hesitated. Asui charged from the ditch and threw me face down at the road's edge. There we lay as the car neared.

We had guerrillas on both sides of the road waiting, with guns fixed on the vehicle. The headlights prevented us from seeing the occupants until the car was even with our position. The vehicle carried two Jap officers. We could hear them chatting as it rolled

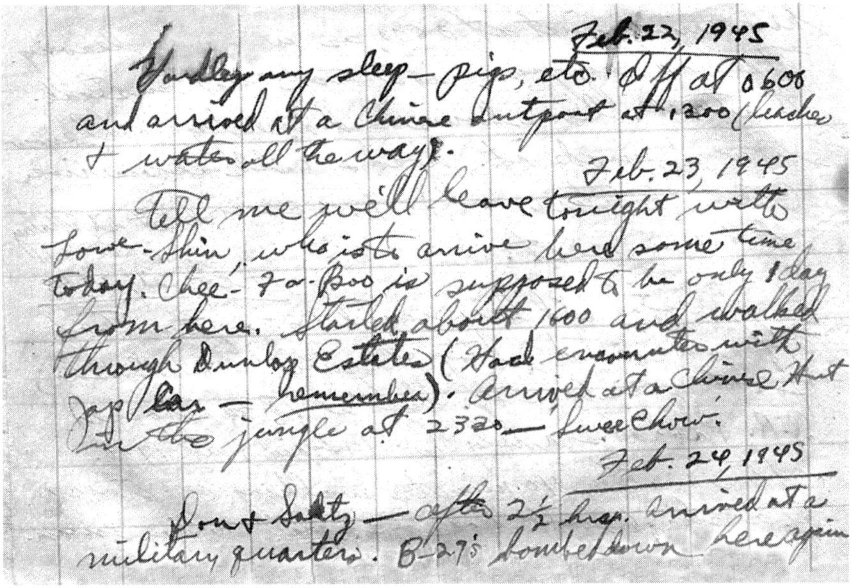

Duffy's diary

Feb. 22, 1945

Hardly any sleep—pigs, etc. Off at 0600 and arrived at a Chinese outpost at 1200 (leaches & water all the way).

Feb. 23, 1945

Tell me we'll leave tonight with Lowe-Shin, who is to arrive here some time today. Chee-Ta-Boo is supposed to be only 1 day from here. Started about 1600 and walked through Dunlop Estates (Had encounter with Jap [illegible] — remember). Arrived at a Chinese Hut in the jungle at 2320 — swell chow.

Feb. 24, 1945

Don & Saltz — after 2½ hrs. arrived at a military quarters. B-29's bombed down here again

Duffy's diary

past and continued up the road.

English Tom helped me to my feet and said, "The men happy they near camp. You frighten them! They eager to end this journey with you."

I looked at the Chinese and they did seem nervous, maybe irritated. Asui shook his head and offered a half smile. I guess my antics tried their patience and rattled their nerves.

The next morning, the final leg of a five-day trek, B-29s flew overhead. I watched in silence. English Tom was quiet—no ridicule this time.

The target had probably been Singapore, and now they were headed home. The sight and sound of the silver bombers encouraged me to continue my fight. *"Hold on, Peggy!"*

I entered Chee-Fa-Pu—Third Division Headquarters—that morning, more dead than alive. I had lost sixty pounds in forty-four days, most of it in the past three weeks, since Carl and I became ill. My skin was marked by scabs, running sores, cuts, bites and swelling. The jungle leeches left their holes about my legs, privates, stomach, back and chest. Most were infected. My legs, swollen from thigh to toe, were nearly twice in size. They were retaining fluids and I feared beriberi. By this time, I was showing symptoms of malaria, cholera, typhoid and beriberi. It did me little good to know how many diseases I was fighting, since there was no medicine, nor nutritious foods, to fight back. My skin and the whites of my eyes had taken on a yellow color. Abdominal cramps, along with watery and bloody diarrhea, signaled some complication of the intestinal system. I had trouble remaining coherent or focused. I was confused and, depending on the fever, often delirious.

I was placed on the sapling bed in the *basha* that Hump and Saltz were assigned to, and passed out. I was out for two days before coming around and seeing Hump and Saltz.

Asui had informed Humphrey and Saltzman about Carl's death, my fight for life, and our journey to Third Division Headquarters. They were amazed that I had survived three weeks with the same sickness that killed Carl in eight days, that I had traveled five days in the roughest jungle terrain, escaped two close brushes with the Japs, and survived a cable-bridge river crossing.

Our conversations were strained in the beginning.

"You bastards left us to save your own butts!" I yelled.

"Duff, we had to go. We were ordered to move on to arrange our escape from Malaya. We had no idea that the orders we received would only mean moving to this camp!" Humphrey said.

"Ordered, Hump? Are you taking orders from the Communists and leaving your men to die?"

"You're out of line, Duff! We couldn't do anything for the two of you," Humphrey said.

"Hump, Carl's dead. Is that the best you can offer? You'll have to live with this for the rest of your life and ask yourself, 'Could I have saved Carl?'"

"Yes, I'll have to live with it," Humphrey answered.

Saltzman started to speak, but I cut him short. "Saltz, don't say a word, just keep quiet!" Humphrey looked at Saltzman and shook his head, signaling him to let it rest, not to provoke this any further.

I would never forget that they left Carl and me, and how Carl died. I would only accept that it happened. This was the best I could do.

We only spoke to each other when it was necessary. It was the second week before the three of us warmed enough to talk.

I kept to myself, bedridden much the time, trying to recover. Humphrey and Saltzman took darn good care of me, feeding, exercising and bathing me.

My legs were still swollen badly. Each day the swelling lessened, though the fever and chills came and went for days on end. The diarrhea eased. They kept me filled with fluids, which they boiled ahead of time to prevent any more parasites or bacteria from entering my body. They tried to secure additional foodstuffs from the commander, Woo Ping, with little success.

Chee-Fa-Pu was deep in the jungle, with only two trails leading in and out of the guerrilla camp. The trails were guarded with machine guns and the camp's clearing was along the swampy shore of Tasek Bera. There were about one hundred Communists living in this camp.

"Duff, you should have been here on our second day," Hump said. I lay on the bamboo mat, which covered our *basha's* mud floor, as Humphrey and Saltzman brought me up to date.

"The second day here, the guerrillas asked Saltz and me to play a game one of them had learned at an English missionary school. So we agreed and joined them in the camp's clearing.

"Well, the game turns out to be 'tag,' and for the next two hours we're running around like kids. There's twelve to fifteen Chinese wearing guns, bullets, grenades, whooping it up, hollering and screaming like school children. Saltz and I were laughing so hard we could hardly stand!" Hump said.

"Hump, how about the social that night and the play they performed?" Saltz said.

"Oh, it was a classic, Duff!" Hump said. "We gather at that large *basha* over there." Hump pointed across the clearing. "They call it the school house, because they hold daily lessons in Communism for the guerrillas, filling them with propaganda.

"We were guests of honor and they seated us in the front row. The actors in the play were all guerrillas, plus Soo Ah, a Chinese girl from Singapore, who was a cabaret singer before joining the Communists."

"There's a woman in this camp who was a cabaret singer?"

"Four women," Saltzman said. "They're as hard as the men of this outfit. Soo Ah wears a grenade on her belt and I think she can take care of herself pretty well."

"Saltz should know, he's tried to woo each woman more than once," Hump said.

Frowning at Saltzman, I said, "Saltz, don't you have any qualms at all?"

"None. I hope to share myself with all of Malaya!"

"I wish I could get a letter off to your mother," I said. Saltz and Hump laughed. "Tell me about the play, Hump."

"It starts with a family at center stage. Husband,

wife and two children, all played by guerrillas. The family can't make ends meet, no food, no money. So the husband says he's going to collaborate with the Japanese. The wife pleads with him not to, but he ignores her. The children plead with him not to, but he ignores them.

"Next, in walks a Jap officer all smiles and shakes hands with the husband. The officer hands money to him and exits. The wife weeps, the children weep.

"Husband leaves to spy on the Communists. Then, in walk some Communists, tall, strong, good friends. The wife tells the Communists that her husband is spying on them for the Japs. The Communists leave.

"Back is the husband, flaunting a new coat, smoking a cigarette, half drunk and bragging about his new life working for the Japs. Wife begins weeping, children begin weeping. In come Communists and husband declares he's innocent. Finally, he confesses and Communists shoot him. Husband falls dead.

"Communists begin singing their 'Internationale' and lift their arms in their clenched-fist salute to the audience, along with the wife and children.

"Afterward, everyone walks off together, smiling and happy. The audience stood up clapping and cheering—they loved it. Duff, this was a real piece of work. We nearly lost it with laughter. If Carl. . . ."

We avoided eye contact, until I broke the silence. "Tell me about this Woo Ping character."

"He's the commander of this camp. A real pleasure to be around. Three days after we get here, Woo Ping arrives," Hump said.

"Pretty bad?" I asked.

Hump nodded his head, agreeing.

"At 0630 there's the blast of a whistle, calling all the guerrillas to attention in the middle of the clearing. They gather their gear and race to get in line before a party of seven guerrillas and Woo Ping enter the camp.

"He's all decked out in a white shirt with gold epaulets sewn on the shoulders and those riding britches that are baggy from the waist to the knee and fit tight from the knee to the ankle. Know what I mean?"

"I'm getting the picture."

"His cap has three red stars on it, he's wearing leggings with blue and white trim and he's got a revolver attached to a braided cord on his belt. This guy looks like the leader of all the Chinese Communists.

"Anyway, he ignores us and proceeds to inspect his troops, yelling at the men because of the way they're holding their guns, or their stance, and giving it to them pretty good.

"I think he meant to impress Saltz and me. Eventually he quits, without even glancing at us, and heads over to that larger *basha* to the right of the school. That's his place all to himself. The other *bashas* hold ten to fifteen men each.

"He drills his men daily, forcing them to march each morning and evening. And he watches from the shade of his *basha*, where it's cooler, while they fight the heat and humidity, out in the sun or drenching rain.

"That night at 2100, he sends English Tom over to invite us to dinner. Saltz, tell Duff about dinner."

Saltzman sat next to me on the bamboo mat and continued the story.

"Duff, we arrive at Woo Ping's *basha* and there's two places set for Hump and me, at one side of the table, with a bowl of rice broth waiting. Sitting on the other side are Woo Ping, Yung Han and English Tom. They have a pot of hot chicken, cooked rice and coffee."

"Yung Han and English Tom?" I asked.

"Yeah, these guys get around. It's hard to know who is who and to what camp they are assigned. Apparently, everyone we've met so far reports to Woo Ping and falls under Third Division Headquarters," Saltzman said.

"Well anyway, English Tom motioned for us to sit down and was so ashamed he wouldn't look at us during dinner. Woo Ping ignored us and continued eating.

"We sipped our broth in silence and then watched Woo Ping finish the last of the chicken and have another cup of coffee.

"Finally, he sits back, lights a cigarette and says to us in pretty good English, 'The Malayan Peoples Anti-Jap Army, doing very well against Japanese. We causing them much grief throughout Malaya, killing officers, burning buildings and trucks, stealing food and weapons.

'The British and Americans, doing terribly against Japanese. Beaten every battle. All ships sinking in sea and airplanes falling from sky, just like you fall from sky.'

"About this time I'm gritting my teeth and ready

to give him what for, when I feel Hump squeeze my wrist under the table. Hump says to him, 'We would like to travel to your Supreme Headquarters. We understand they have a radio, which we can use to contact the Allies and arrange for our escape from Malaya.'"

"Woo Ping says, 'You must write letter asking permission to go to Headquarters.' Hump says, 'We've already written a letter to your Headquarters quite some time ago.' So, good old Ping says, 'That not matter, you must write another letter.' That was the end of dinner. Woo Ping stood up and motioned for us to leave his *basha*!"

"Well, he sounds like a lovely guy. I can't wait to meet him," I said.

Saltz continued, "The following morning a Chinese boy races in here and says that Woo Ping sent orders for us to hurry to his *basha*. We were still hopeful the commander would be friendly, so we made our way to him.

"We entered and waited ten minutes, while he sat behind a desk and never looked up. He was reading what appeared to be a newspaper or propaganda letter of some sort. Finally, he stared at us with cold eyes and rudely asked, 'Is Russia good or bad?'

"We couldn't believe our ears! Here's a guerrilla commander sitting in the midst of a swamp lake, surrounded by thick jungle, asking our opinion of Russia. Hump took a chance and replied, 'Our country regards Russia as our ally in the war.' Woo didn't like Hump's answer. He scowled, ignoring us again as he shuffled stacks of pamphlets together and

placed them neatly on the table in front of us. There
was a hammer and sickle on the outside page, so we
could imagine the Communist propaganda on the
inside. I wanted to lift one, but the opportunity didn't
exist.

"Hump asks him, 'What is that thick book in
front of you?' Woo says, 'This Russian manual teaches
guerrilla tactics.' Then he opens a book containing a
map of the United States and says, 'Where your
homes?' Hump points to the blazing metropolis of
Postville, population twelve, in northeast Iowa."
Hump and I laughed quietly and Saltz continued.

"I pointed to Washington, D.C., which seemed
to make him uneasy. Then he asked Hump about
yours and Carl's home. Hump pointed to Los Angeles
for Carl and Chicago for you. This aroused Woo.
He says, 'Chicago good city, many Communists live
Chicago.' He didn't tell us how he came to believe that
many Communists live in Chicago. When you get
home, Duff, you should look into that and see that
they join Woo Ping here in the jungle. This would be
a wonderful place for all of them. Disease, mosquitoes,
leeches, starvation."

Hump continued the story. "Woo Ping then took
off in a lesson on the wonderful life the Communists
will provide, once the Malayan people are liberated from
the capitalist British and the imperialistic Japanese.

"He tells us, 'Communists will provide work for
all Malayans, each will have equal wages, each will
have equal food, clothes and homes. Free schools for
everyone, all patriots to Communist party. I have six
years school,' bragged Woo Ping. 'Each person will

have six years school from Communists. Can you say your country this generous to your people?'"

"I knew I had to be careful with how I handled this question, but he deserved my answer. With a straight face I said quietly, 'In the United States our government provides each American twelve years of free school.' Woo slammed his book and said, 'You will stay here at Third Division Headquarters until I have talked with our Supreme Leader. You must not leave camp, you must give me your guns, there must be no talk of America with my comrades and you must go to school each day to learn many wonderful things of our party.'"

"I still think this is why we were restricted to our *basha*, Hump!" Saltzman said. "Woo Ping said it was for our protection."

"Not allowed out of the *basha*?" I asked.

"That was for three days, until Woo Ping left for a few days, but he didn't enforce it after he returned," Hump said.

"What about the guns? Why did he let you keep the guns?"

"I told Woo Ping, 'We will not give you our weapons until we reach Supreme Headquarters.' Woo Ping said we would be allowed to keep them temporarily."

"Seems everyone is hell-bent on taking our guns. What about the school 'to learn many wonderful things of the Communist Party?'"

"We haven't enrolled yet and Woo Ping hasn't named us truant," Saltz said.

"English Tom keeps us up to date with news.

He heard our boys are taking over the Philippines and Singapore is getting hit regularly by our B-29s," Hump said.

"They're stepping things up," I answered.

"Looks like they're beginning to take back the South Pacific."

"I hope so!"

"Hump, at times I don't know if I'm going to make it. It's been a month since I got ill. I can't shake this thing. Each time the fever hits, I'm weaker and I don't know if it's the beginning of the end. I need a doctor and medicine."

"English Tom said there is a doctor who lives on a rubber plantation near here," Hump said. "We'll press Woo Ping to get you some help. It appears Woo Ping is under orders to look after us. He's been the same bastard all along, but he pretty much leaves us alone. I think he answers to someone as detestable as himself."

That evening, Woo Ping said he would take me to an Indian doctor if I could walk five hours.

The following day we got started at 1100—Woo Ping, four guards and me. We stopped at a Chinese outpost in mid-afternoon for food and rest, and finally arrived at 2100. My slow pace doubled the time.

Woo Ping and I grasped handguns as we crept through the plantation in the darkness, reaching the back door of the doctor's home.

Woo Ping tapped on the door with the nose of his gun. The door opened and a slender, dark-skinned man looked at our guns and us.

"Good evening. May I help you?"

"You speak English," I said.

"Yes. You are one of the Americans from the airplane, aren't you?"

"Yes, I am. How did you know?"

"Most people know of your plane crash. The Japanese have said a great deal about how their superior fighting destroyed the airship and killed those responsible for killing innocent women and children. They hope to have us side with them, by telling us lies. But Malayans know that the Americans are our friends and allies." The words lifted my spirit and I smiled.

Woo Ping interrupted and spoke harshly to the doctor in Chinese. The middle-aged man invited us in and led us down a dimly lit hallway, past rooms with beds occupied by Malay, Chinese, or Indian patients. He used his home as a hospital.

We entered what appeared to be an examination room and the doctor pulled the shade on each window. He lit a lamp and raised its wick, illuminating the room. Closing the door, he motioned for me to take a seat alongside a table holding various instruments, gauze, cotton, ointment and antiseptics.

Woo Ping seated himself near one of the windows, peering out from time to time into the dark. He and I kept our weapons in hand.

"You are safe here!" the doctor assured. "What is troubling you?"

Just then the door flew open and a man entered, letting out a hair-raising scream! I fell to the floor, dropped the .45 and struggled to retrieve it, then glanced back at the door. Woo Ping hit the floor and hid behind a chair. The man bolted from the room, slamming the door!

Shaken, I screamed, "What was that?"

The doctor answered, "Please relax, everything is okay."

"Who was that?" I insisted.

"Pay no attention to him, the man is crazy."

"He scared the hell out of me! I'm shaking," I said in a nervous voice. "What's the matter with him?"

"He is insane, but not violent."

"Not violent! I would hate to see him violent."

Woo Ping slowly got to his feet, spoke to the doctor and headed to the door. He opened it slowly, and peered down the dim hallway in both directions. He looked at the doctor and me, then left the room, closing the door behind him.

"Where's he going?" I asked.

"He will wait for you at the edge of the jungle. It appears he is afraid to remain here."

"And I am afraid to remain here!" I said. I clutched the .45 in my right hand.

The doctor smiled and said, "What can I do for you, my friend?"

I described the symptoms: fever, chills, vomiting, diarrhea, swelling. I spoke of Carl and his death. The doctor had me take off the upper part of my ragged flight suit and listened to my lungs and heart rhythm. I relaxed as the examination continued.

The door flew open again and a frightful scream filled the room! I stopped short of firing my gun as the door crashed shut. My heart pounded and my pulse raced.

"That guy is making me a nervous wreck . . . he

does that again and I'm likely to shoot him!"

The doctor smiled and continued his examination. He cleaned, applied antiseptic and covered many badly infected leech holes.

"You must be more careful of the jungle leech. Check your skin frequently when there is water on your path."

I thought the advice was humorous. "I'm living in water, Doc!"

"Your condition is poor. You must watch your diet and you should start eating better food."

I thought, what a laugh, better food. Rice and rice broth everyday.

"The red patches on your skin is ringworm. Your abdominal pain and cramps, along with the diarrhea, has me suspect a bacteria traveling through your digestive tract and maybe your bloodstream. It can settle in your liver, kidney, gallbladder or heart. This may be cholera or typhoid fever, both are similar in symptoms. The yellow color of your skin and the whites of your eyes is an infection of the liver or gallbladder. You also have a slight case of malaria."

"Can you help me? Can you give me any medicine to fight back?" I asked.

"If you stay here and let me tend to you, I can help."

"I can't stay here, it's not safe. Even you would be in danger. The Japs would kill us both."

"Yes, but I cannot do much if you leave." The good doctor paused and said, "I can get you medicine, but it will take five days' time. The Communists will have to send a runner for it. You must get rest and watch what you eat. Boil all your drinking and cooking water."

The screamer was back, hollering and slamming the door, upending my nerves and irritating my stomach.

"I want to shoot him. Can I shoot him?" I asked the doctor. He just smiled.

"I will send MacLean's Powder, a quinine mixture, and treatment for the ringworm. You should take the cure for the ringworm before taking the quinine mixture. There will be directions to follow."

Before I departed, the kind doctor served me chicken curry, vegetables, and gave me four books in English. A history of St. Matthew, an adventure story, a geography of Asia and a collection of famous English diaries. Each book was missing several pages, which natives had removed to roll cigarettes. This was our only reading material and we enjoyed them again and again.

In the days ahead, I rested and took good care of myself. Rice was the only food and never enough. But Woo Ping continued to eat well—plenty of chicken and coffee for him.

Although he preached equality within the Communist party, it was he who continually breached his words. Time and again, he had the only cigarettes, soap, shoes, socks, clean clothes, wine, coffee and chicken. The man was a fraud!

In one instance, English Tom was a victim of Woo Ping's cruelty. Tom had become a dear friend and treated Hump, Saltz and me well. He tended to simple needs that made life more tolerable. In thanks for the kindness, we presented to him Carl Hansman's watch as a gift. He was extremely gracious and moved by our generosity. One hour later, Woo Ping was wearing Carl's watch and a wounded Tom was wearing Woo Ping's old watch. I felt Tom's pain and I wanted to destroy Woo Ping.

Yung Han fell victim also. He was well liked and the local natives and farmers presented him with a Malayan Communist flag. It was made by some of the farmers' wives and was bright red with three gold stars. All these people had written sentiments and signed the flag. Yung Han was brought to tears by their kindness. Woo Ping broke out in laughter on seeing the emotion of the courteous and grateful Yung Han. He tore the flag from his hands and tossed it to one of the Chinese girls and ordered her to make socks. Yung Han was furious, as were the guerrillas, but none dared challenge the heartless commander.

I spent most days laid up in our *basha*. I pushed myself to exercise a little each day, eager to gain strength for our trip to Communist Headquarters. Otherwise, I lay around listening to exotic birds and insects, reading and working on diary entries to pass time.

March 6, 1945—Brother Bob's birthday today. I wonder how many more I'll see go by, before leaving Malaya? Hope he finally got home, that will be some consolation for the folks. Hope Peg is over most of the shock & suffering (Hold on honey, I'll be back).

We three had lovely food today, the white potato that killed all the Aussies and a lot of other crap. We are starved & the Doc told me to watch my diet what a laugh.

March 9, 1945—The commander came back last night, after walking 16 hours (he claims). He stated that the Russians were in Berlin and that the Americans were fighting in Cologne. It won't be long if that's true.

Americans are also supposed to have occupied the Volcano Islands and the Philippines are now completely occupied. Roosevelt, Churchill and Stalin were supposed to have met in the Crimean area. . . .

Plenty of Jap cigs floating around since Woo Ping's return. Today they opened a contribution box, which they placed in the schoolhouse. They did quite well, considering these soldiers only get paid $4 Jap money each month. Woo Ping stood by, watching as each guerrilla passed the box and made his deposit. Not much of a choice on how to spend their $4 Jap money.

Missed a social tonight. Got chills, fever, and nauseated feeling again . . . Took quinine & hit sack.

March 11, 1945—Had another bad spell. This was the worse day I've had since landing. Found blood again in bowel passage and suffering from intense cramps. Chills, fever, couldn't eat, vomiting, plenty of quinine and this is the two month anniversary in Malaya . . . still no medicine.

Russians not in Berlin as we were told, but they are surrounding it. Americans now 20 miles east of Rhine past Cologne.

Woo Ping told us that the Japs had killed over two hundred Malays in Kampong Kota, near Tampin, where we bailed out of the Postville Express. Snakes!

The next day, Yung Han and ten others arrived, reporting to Woo Ping. He didn't wait long to grill and drill the poorly nourished men, up and down the clearing, parading for hours in searing heat and humidity with no water.

I would lie on a grass mat on the *basha* floor, perspiring in the shade, while men collapsed throughout the afternoon, only to be revived and marched again.

Woo Ping was demented. How could one treat his troops with such cruelty? You would think that these men were his prisoners, rather than comrades. But their military mastery was not adequate enough for Woo Ping; he expected perfection.

Ten days after my visit to the doctor the medicine arrived. The worm treatment wasn't sent. Eighty-five dollars for five aspirin tablets; on the box it stated ten-cents for six. One hundred dollars for twenty-five powders of MacLean's medicine for stomach disorder. Some people see war as opportunity for profit. The good doctor requested no payment, but someone was racketeering. I stayed on the quinine to try to knock out the malaria first, and then used the Mac's Powder.

Finally, news arrived by runner. We were anxious to hear Supreme Headquarters' response to our request. Woo Ping waited another day before sharing the news.

"You are permitted to leave Chee-Fa-Pu," Woo Ping stated with a smile. He handed Hump the note. We were instructed by the Commander of the Third Regiment to proceed to his camp.

"English Tom, where is Third Regiment or Su-Ling-Pu located?" Hump asked.

"Many days south. You must cross Muar River."

"So much for heading north," Saltz griped. "Hope there's ladies."

I entered Woo Ping's quarters. Seated at his desk, he glanced up but continued shuffling papers, forcing me to wait until he acknowledged my presence. His arrogance was visible in every action.

Looking up, he waved his hand and sat back in his chair.

"Woo Ping, I came for my gun. We're ready to leave for Su-Ling-Pu." He had taken my .45 during my bout with fever, stating I had no need for a gun.

"I keep the gun!" Woo Ping answered.

"I need the gun for our trip through the jungle!"

"The Anti-Jap Army needs gun!"

"Woo Ping, we have promised to turn all our guns over to your brave and loyal Anti-Jap Army once we depart Malaya. We have signed a paper for your people."

"I have this gun, you may leave!"

"What is it you want for my gun, Woo Ping?"

Woo Ping pondered my offer. I did not intend to go unarmed with Japs, tigers, wild boars, snakes and who knows what sharing jungle trails.

"I give you gun, you give me coat."

"Oh shit!" I mumbled.

Outside, I checked my weapon and Humphrey commented, "Good job, Duff, how did you do it?"

"I had to give the peter my flight jacket!"

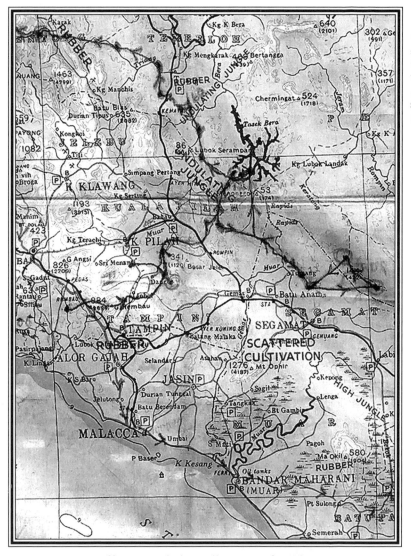

Duffy carried this silk map of Malaya,
marking each spot they camped or stayed,
as they walked barefoot through the jungle.

Su-Ling-Pu

At O810 on March 18, 1945, we departed. Woo Ping didn't come out of his *basha* to say good-bye, which was fine with us. We hated him!

During our farewell, the guerrillas gave us gifts of Jap money, cigarettes and reading materials. Many of these men thought we held high positions in our government and we saw no reason to tell them different. It meant better treatment and possibly our lives. We couldn't be sure we would hold the same value otherwise.

English Tom said, "I will miss you, my friends. I know you will go home to your family. This I am sure. Please remember me!"

"Thank you for everything, Tom," I replied, embracing him. "I will miss you, too! Thank Yung Han and Asui, and tell them we're sorry we missed them."

Hump and Saltz finished their good-byes and we shoved off behind three Communist escorts, Na Tom, Chang and Sung Fu.

Na Tom maintained a fast pace and we named him "Speedy." Sulky-looking man with a bucktooth, who made it clear he hated all white men. He was another who despised the harsh rule of the British, trusting only those with yellow or brown skin.

Our bearer, Sung Fu, had open lesions on his arms and legs. Some skin disease that looked unfriendly. He would pick and squeeze them, and use his spit to wash them. We looked at anything but him when he doctored himself.

Chang spoke English. He was groomed, friendly, and did not seem to care much for his comrades, so we liked him.

"Woo Ping sure picked a couple fine boys," I said to Hump and Saltz.

"Don't you know it! I wonder if they know their way," Hump whispered. "Woo Ping probably planned it this way."

March 19, 1945—The first day we trekked five hours. The last two and a half hours we blazed the trail and it was plenty rough. We reached a Chinese outpost and had a horrible night's sleep with bloodthirsty mosquitoes.

Up at 0530, rice and on the road at 0635. Rain nearly the whole trip and fern leaves our only protection. Plenty of bamboo to sidestep and battle, or squeeze your body through its narrow spaces. Received leech bites all over my body from these bastards. Crossed about five rivers or streams via the log method. Washed out underclothes and now wondering if they'll dry out. Snafu.

March 20, 1945—The usual night's sleep and up at 0600. Clothes didn't dry as I suspected. Hump has a swollen eye from a spider bite and my left eye is the same way. Saltzman is immune to everything—it must be his sour nature.

Left at 1000 with one addition to the party, a girl who carried food, etc. on a hoe. How she carried this load is beyond me. Leeches all the way. Marshland and mud is the only description for this leg of the trip.

Our guide forgot his pack at the first resting place, so he had to travel back up the trail one hour. The girl took over the lead—not so good. We crossed over at least 60 logs and waded across a few streams . . . Rain keeps coming and when it subsides mosquitoes and other pests attack. Not sure which is worse . . . haven't been dry for four days.

March 22, 1945—Off at 0840 and arrived 1210 at another outpost. Leeches added more open sores to our bodies. We crossed a Chinese compound and Chang purchased a side of pig, and brother we really ate two delicious meals. All the Chinese are good cooks and can take damn good care of themselves—remarkable considering the life.

A Malay came over with his family and presented us with a mouse deer. The Chinese wouldn't accept the gift and insisted on giving them $2—I guess they don't want to have any obligation when they try to take over this country. . . .

Saw many wild animal tracks, elephant, boar and cat. Traveled through quite a few clearings or grassy areas, ideal for cats. Everyone nervous . . . Rain keeps coming and clouds of mosquitoes are devouring us.

March 24, 1945—Up at 0535, rain all night and

still coming. Played with the snails while waiting for the rain to subside.

Off at 1050 with Speedy in the lead. Water on the trail and plenty of wild animal tracks. Saw a horde of wild boar, but they were as frightened as we were. After wading hip deep in umpteen streams, we really came to a honey. Turns out we had been in floodwater from the Muar River for over an hour, and now we were nearing the river itself.

The Chinese pointed out we must swim across the main channel of the river and boasted what good swimmers they were, but worried about our chances. So, we worried!

The Chinese built a raft for all the equipment, which got saturated, and we swam in GI boots. Saltz lost a boot, which Hump somehow managed to rescue. As we made the crossing, we found ourselves having to hold the raft up to keep it from sinking and killing snakes attempting to climb from the murky water.

Just as the water reached our necks, the Chinese began to scream and holler at us.

"What the hell are they yelling about, Hump?"

"Damned if I know, Duff!"

I looked at Chang and yelled, "What are they saying, Chang?"

"They say, 'We are drowning, please save us!'"

So much for "good swimmers." Hump and I found ourselves rescuing both the Chinese and our gear, which was constantly falling off the top-heavy raft. Our guns fell in several times—how we didn't lose one amazes me. I shook all the way across and helped, as I was able. This ordeal lasted for an hour.

On the other side, our Chinese friends acted as

if it was business as usual, until Hump tore into them. "You could have gotten us all killed out there!" Chang translated. "What stupidity! Why brag of how good a swimmer you are, when you can't swim a lick?"

I started laughing and Saltz joined me. I couldn't believe they boasted of how well they could swim in one moment, only to damn near drown in the next.

"Chinese honor at stake, never show you not master, more honorable to die!" Chang said.

Hump, shaking his head from side to side, looked at Saltz and me bursting with laughter and cracked up too. The insanity of it made us laugh all the harder.

This served as a reminder anytime the guerrillas claimed to be experts at anything, which was quite common. They always felt it necessary to be one up on the other. They found it most difficult to admit they were lost or unsure of a path they chose to follow. They would rather circle around and end up back in the place they had been two hours earlier. Not knowing where they were headed, we couldn't lend help, which they "never need" anyway. Everywhere we went was a secret. Jungle treks took longer because they were never quite sure how to get somewhere, and were too proud to ask.

"We have leeches!" I announced. "Got one on my wrist!" I pulled at the engorged body and flipped it into the muddy water.

"I have them on my arm!" Saltz said. "Let's stop and get these bastards off, they're probably all over us."

Humphrey grabbed Speedy's shoulder and signaled him to stop. We helped each other remove leeches, but from our waist down we stood in muddy water. Those would have to wait until later.

Waist deep, our feet buried in muck, we could feel reptiles bumping against our legs. We kicked, splashed, and yelled to keep them away. Fear of alligators and snakes replaced our dread of the leeches. It was odd—we were afraid of anything under the water, even though it might be only a stick, branch, or fish. The unknown made us anxious and fed our fear.

Rain hushed the chatter of the jungle's birds and animals. The sound of the rain on a canopy of leaves took me back to the front porch of 8132 Wood Street, Chicago. Peggy and I sat close on the porch swing and listened to the evening downpour, as we whispered . . . *"Bill, I'm frightened I'll lose you, that you won't make it back. I'm scared to death that Danny and our baby will grow up without a father to hug, kiss, and love them. I can't shake these thoughts. Too many people have died in this horrible war. Friends, relatives, classmates, neighbors. So many, never coming home. All this death, bloodshed, and killing—I hate the war! I'm scared, Bill!"*

"Peggy, I'll be back, believe me! No matter what happens, I'll be back . . . I promise you, Red!" Our embrace sent heat through our bodies. We held each other tight, trading kisses in the rain. . . .

"Duff, you okay?" Hump was shaking me. I had stopped and was grasping a fern branch. Rain dripped from my face and I stared into emptiness. I focused on Hump and answered.

"Yeah, I'm okay. Just tired, Hump. Real tired. My fever is back and this swamp is tough going."

The endless rain, mud, swamp and thick jungle were too much. We quit and took refuge at a deserted compound, hoping the rain would end. Each man had leech bites over his entire lower body. We couldn't make a fire with wet wood and grass, which meant no dry clothes or heat to cease our shivering.

March 25, 1945—Most miserable sleep I've ever spent in my life. My blanket was soaking wet from the trip. I was given one that just covered my stomach, and consequently mosquitoes bit the hell out of me the whole night. Hope to push on despite rain.

Country we are traveling through now is a lot different. Ferns, coconut trees, orchards, lime trees, bananas, and plenty of coffee beans. Informed we couldn't leave for a while, since the water is over our head again—Lovely! Our progress gets slower, but getting more used to it every day.

Plenty of trouble with the monkeys stealing our food. Hump and I were trying to get one, but no luck. Wish I knew something about ornithology, because the birds in Malaya are really unique. The insects are plentiful and the different types keep one guessing. Govednik would really enjoy this atmosphere. I wonder how many of the four men captured are still alive. Rumor has it that they weren't being fed and three out of four had died or been killed.

Never did mention the curious methods they have for curing people who get sick. One fellow at Woo Ping's had something like an epileptic fit, so they called the cook and he breaks a bottle and cuts small holes in the fellow's head—I guess they were bleeding him. Surprisingly, the next day he was marching with the troops.

Another had trouble with his stomach, so they set fire to a piece of paper, put it on his stomach with a coin on top and placed a small shot glass over this. They said they were taking the air out—what shit!

Have seen about 15 fellows with infected legs, some that look like cancerous sores, all from leech bites. They treat them with herbs and ashes, and for some reason they nearly always get better—remarkable!

Most of these people have malaria and different types of fever from drinking out of stagnant jungle pools, but it doesn't kill or bother them—quinine and cholera medicine take care of all the illnesses. Feel more confident each day that I'll get back. Hold on, Peg darling!

After one day, my fever quit. I gained a bit of strength and we continued.

We reached another outpost and huddled around the fire, feeding on rice and hot tea. I listened to Chang, the English-speaking character. His humor was good medicine and I liked his company. He was educated and expressed interest in the United States, our way of life and our government. He told us, "Before the occupation my family farmed a ten-acre rubber estate, which the Japs took. I joined the guerrillas because of the Japs' demand to serve them. If I had stayed in Kuala Lumpur, I would be a soldier for the Japs or my head would be on display. So I slipped away one evening and was introduced to the Communist guerrillas."

In the morning Chang, Speedy and Sung Fu departed, heading back to their camp. We were always saying goodbye to the guerrillas. The Communist system did not permit them to travel beyond a few camps. It was a "Pony Express" operation, with a security measure to protect camps from being given away by traitors and deserters, tired of the jungle and harsh treatment of their officers, which was common. We were like a letter being passed from post to post. *April 1, 1945—Quite a number of girls at this outpost. Saltz, after spending last night with a girl he blessed with a child, was in a rare mood today. Our differences grow. Rain lighter . . . Left - 0700 - for Su-Ling-Pu with new guards and walked two and a half hours without rest. Rough going! Climbed many hills and traveled unsteady trail all the way. Many trying experiences with logs and wading through water over our hips. But we arrived at Su-Ling-Pu, ending fourteen days of misery and fatigue.*

"Greetings Americans, I am Ko Shing. Welcome to Third Regiment Headquarters!"

"Ko Shing, where are we?" Hump asked.

"Twenty-five miles northeast Segamat, along Keratong River."

I charted our course on my map. It was seventy miles from Kampong Istana Raja, where we bailed out, to the shores of Tasek Bera and Chee-Fa-Pu. Now, we were forty miles southeast of Chee-Fa-Pu and seventy-five miles due east from where we bailed out. Yet our journey had covered approximately 130 miles of the Malayan jungle since landing. Oh, my aching back. . . .

There were two captains, Ah Sing and Woo Coo Shing—both young men—following a precedent that had prevailed throughout the whole organization. The young are more impressionable, less grounded and unaware of the Communists' true motive. Easily influenced, they swallow the Communists' hook. We asked Ah Sing about our future.

"You stay in Malaya until liberated! We fight war

with Jap. We have no radio here to contact outside world. Our news travels outpost to outpost with runner. I know my duty to get you back, but this not possible. We feed you, give you *basha* and protect you!"

"Ah Sing, we have written letters to Supreme Headquarters. Have they received any of our letters?" Hump asked.

"This I not know. You write again and Supreme Headquarters will get all information."

"Here we go again!" Saltz said.

Learning that we were to live out the war in the Malayan jungle was disturbing. I was in poor health, only a stone's throw away from the illness that had killed Carl, and the medicine cabinet was bare. But in another way, I felt secure, because we were deep within the jungle out of harm's way.

The camp was large, with over one hundred people making up the garrison. There was a clearing, where parading and marching took place each morning. Five *bashas* stood along one edge of the clearing, out of aerial view of Jap planes searching for the Communists' camps. Each *basha* housed roughly twenty Chinese on one sapling bed. The schoolhouse where lessons in Communism and evening socials were held—where we sang often—was across the clearing from the *bashas*. The commanders' quarters, each with their own beds, were next to the school.

The leaders always preached equality, though it never included food, clothes, cigarettes, soap, weapons, sleep, medicine, exercise, or marching. But none dared challenge their lies.

The days ahead were monotonous, with little to

do except swim, read or journal and hope for news.

April 6, 1945—The Americans are in Hamburg. Frankfort occupied in the east by Russians and west by Americans. German government has moved to Munich and it looks like the end is near. Americans have taken Palawan in the Philippines and have made landings in the Ryukyu Islands North of Formosa. Mandalay captured in Burma and Tokyo a blaze of fire, twenty-four miles completely devastated. "When is John Bull coming to Malaya?"

I hope I can get back to Peg and the little ones before the end of this year. Peg must be nearly over the shock by now . . . at least I hope so. I love her more each day of my life. We'll make the grade, Peg honey, keep up your hope and the prayers, your confidence is all I need.

We ate a reptile that looked like a small crocodile. It tasted like chicken, had four claw feet and a forked tongue. It took two rifle shots to kill the bugger. Saw a five-foot brown and green striped snake in the river. It had a fish, about a foot long, half swallowed. Lovely!

"Have you met Sakai?" Foo Yin asked, during an evening bull session. Foo Yin was a young lad who loved to speak English. He became our shadow.

"No, tell us about the Sakai, Foo Yin," I said.

"Oh, Sakai is idol of Chinese. Most jungle clearings where we make camp have been made by Sakai. They control jungle. They wear little clothes and sleep on ground without blanket."

"On the ground?"

"Oh yes, this true! They call monkeys and kill them with blowgun. Eat tiger and elephant meat. Terror to most animals. Spear fish and snake in river and have jungle magic. Gardens and farms never troubled by animals or birds. They go farm and say Sakai words and crops never spoil."

Hump steered the discussion elsewhere. "Foo Yin, there are many captains here. Some we have seen at other camps. How many camps are there?"

"Captains from middle posts here for training. Third Regiment Headquarters have twelve middle posts and five small camps under all middle post. Malaya have eight Regiment Headquarters and Supreme Headquarters." Foo Yin freely shared information about the Communists and their propaganda, along with our friend Dit Swan.

Dit Swan had appeared at our *basha* one afternoon when I was down with fever and asked for a favor. "Lieutenant Bill, I bring you nine points of Communist party. This, I do for you to tell your countrymen in America. Also, I ask you present to your government."

Dit Swan was an honest and sincere young man. Since our arrival he had shown us kindness and friendship.

"Tell me the nine points of the Communist party, Dit Swan." I lay on our sapling bed, killing insects and bugs, as he read the paper aloud.

"The Anti-Japs' Program of the Malayan
Communist party"
1) Drive the Japanese Fascists out of Malaya
and establish the Malayan Republic.
2) Establish a national organization composed
of representatives universally elected from
the different nationalities, to govern and
protect our Motherland, practice people's

sovereignty, improve civilians' living
conditions and develop industry, agricul-
ture, and commerce in order to build up
Malaya as a harmonious free and felici-
tous country.

3) Give freedom of speech, publishing, organization and thought. Abolish all the old
oppressive laws and release all prisoners
and Anti-Jap captives.

4) Improve people's living conditions, relieve
the unemployed and the refugees, increase
wages and salaries, abolish high and
unnecessary taxation and high-interest
money lending.

5) Alter and reorganize the Malayan Anti-
Jap guerrillas into the National Army of
Defense, which will defend our territory.
Bestow special care upon the Anti-Jap
Soldiers and assist the families of those
warriors who died for the liberty of Malaya,
relieve the wounded and disabled soldiers.

6) Free education will be practiced universally in the various national languages,
by the different nationalities in order to
develop National Culture.

7) Confiscate the German, Italian and
Japanese fascists' and traitors' properties,
which will be national properties. Return
the properties confiscated by the Japs to
their original owners providing they are
people of Malaya or people of our friendly
nations.

> *8) Practice autonomy of tariff, sign friendly*
> *agreements and establish commercial relations*
> *with friendly countries.*
>
> *9) Combine with Russia and China and*
> *support the struggles for independence of*
> *the oppressed nations in the Far East, give*
> *help to the Japanese people to fight against*
> *the fascists.*

"Lt. Bill, these points will make Malaya better nation. Nation free of oppression by outsiders. We shall rise up and sweep the land of their injustice."

Young lads like Dit Swan represented truth and hope for their people and Malaya. It's sad that they had been taken in by the deceit and lies of the Communists. The British sure had made a mess for themselves.

"I will take the nine points, Dit Swan, and bring them to America. But, please remember one thing. Outside influence from your new friend, Soviet Russia, has a motive too. Why else would they be so eager to encourage you to fight the British? Notice how their support comes in the form of propaganda advocating not just a free democratic nation, but also a Communist nation. This is *their* choice, not the choice of the people of Malaya."

Dit Swan's face crinkled as he processed my words. I hoped the bit of advice I offered would help him see clearly that Communism disguised itself like a wolf in sheep's clothing.

April 19, 1945—Bad earache in my right ear, too much swimming in the river. Been constantly aching for two days and my sleep at night is miserable. It seems like I go from one illness to another since landing in Malaya.

April 22, 1945—Two years and eight months ago today, I married that gorgeous redhead of mine . . . couldn't think of anything except that it was Saturday night in the States and wondered about Peg. I certainly hope I make it back in time for our third anniversary, August 22.

Ear is still terrible and now have a sore throat in addition. Trying to stay away from a cold and fever that has been trying to catch me.

April 24, 1945—My birthday today . . . Happy birthday Willie! May you be a better man and enjoy your 25th year—there is plenty of room for improvement, you might just as well start today. I certainly missed Peg on my last two birthdays, because she would always have something planned and the day would be most enjoyable.

I look forward to my coming year with delight, for I know my redhead will make up for these days. I believe it is like Ko Shing told me tonight, with Peg. "She knows I'm alive, so there is no use fretting." I know it would relieve her mind though, if I were able to send a message informing her of it. Well, it won't be long and we'll be together permanently.

April 25, 1945—Well, the 'World Peace Conference' starts today in San Francisco and how I would like to be there to see all those notables. A Japanese newspaper came today and told of President Roosevelt's death. If this is true, God help the United States.

I don't know much about Truman except that he is strictly a politician and was part of the Prendergast machine in Kansas City . . . hope Truman has enough brains to drop the ties of the machine and surround himself with some good advisors when he attends this peace conference. Otherwise, Uncle Joe (Stalin) and The (British)

Empire will steal our shirts after we practically carried the world on our shoulders as far as supplies are concerned and have done more than our share of the fighting. Russia would be in German or Japanese hands today, if it wasn't for America's terrific show in the Pacific Theater. News also told of Germans killing 321,000 Russian prisoners—rats!

Ko Shing told us that he thinks Americans will be allowed to have three or four wives after the war, because of all the men being killed—I wonder what the redhead will say to that.

When Woo Coo Shing returned, he told us he wanted to have a meeting with us. Ko Shing, Ah Hong, Dit Swan and practically the whole camp came to our *basha* about 1700. Coffee and soft-boiled eggs made up the menu for the evening. Woo Shing presided and Dit Swan translated.

"You will go home to America! It is arranged for you to journey to Supreme Headquarters. Plans made to evacuate you from Malaya," Woo Shing said with a smile.

Hump, Saltz and I stared at one another; stunned and uncertain. We turned back to Woo Shing and he continued.

"In envelope everything explained." He passed an envelope to Hump, who was sitting between Saltz and me. Hump pulled out two letters and we read them together.

> *Negri Sembilan Communist Party*
> *Officer of Propaganda Dept.*
> *5 April 1945*
> *Dear American Air Flyers,*
> *Our letter introduces American like you. This*

American is friendly with 6th Guerrilla Regiment where he meets you after your arrival.
We must remind you of promise you make with letter giving Communists your pistols for our fight with Jap fascists. This letter you sign before and now you must honor this promise. A soldier's promise is promise. Powerful guerrilla troops to escort you and deliver you 6th Guerrilla Regiment safe. American then meet you. Must remember promise with pistols and good soldier's honor.

Comrade Ah Chek

We looked at each other, but kept our thoughts secret. Every Communist is after the guns. As things stand now, we don't have the guns. We were relieved of them soon after our arrival here, but told we could have them back whenever we wished. Ah Sing had one, but we weren't sure if the other two were even in camp.

Hump opened the other letter and we read over his shoulder in silence.

January 20, 1945

Dear Fellow Countrymen,

On the 11 Jan., I had the thrill of seing six B-29s fly over my headquarters. The sun was not out or else I would have flashed to you with a mirror. I said at the time, that if any of you ever had the misfortune of crashing in this place, that you would crash near me. But last night, I got the bad news that you did crash land and over 100 miles away at that. If this letter reaches you, as I hope it will, it

will introduce to you men from the Sixth Guarilla Regiment. You are in the Sencond Guarilla Regiment's area, but these men will bring you to me. Do not be too suspicious of them, as they have been sent by me. I have instructed them to bring you here by the safest way, so you will probably have a three week hike. I have already radiod South East Asia Command, of the efforts to rescue you and they will arrange a submarine pick up for you. So with luck we should have you out of here in about six weeks, during your stay here it will be my great pleasure to be your guest, I say guest becoz I have not seen or talked to an American for many weeks. So when you get here, I'll throw a big feast for you, and believe it or not there will be wine. I am enclosing a frat card, as an assurance to you that everything is O.K. Please follow these men, as they know the safest way of bringing you to me. In about two weeks, I'll come to meet you halfway, and bring you here myself, at the present it is impossible for me to come. As you con will imagine, I'd like to shoot the bull with you, but that will have to wait till we get together over a bottle of wine. For security reasons my name is cut from the frat card, and I am using a cover name, so don't become alarmed.
    J. Jack Bussey
    C.O. Allied Detachment, U.S. Army
"If that guy is commanding officer of that outfit, he won his commission in a raffle!" Saltz joked.

"This guy can't spell or write! Makes me wonder if he's really an American," Hump said.

"Yeah, the spelling is pathetic," I whispered. "It sounds like Bartholomew or Hollywood, but why would the Communists pull this? Just to get us to turn over our guns? My other hunch says it's the Japs!"

"Yeah, me too, Duff. Could be a Jap spy setting a trap to capture or ambush us," Hump said.

"If this is on the level, he has a radio and said he contacted Southeast Asia Command about picking us up with a submarine. Our ticket home!" I said.

"Hey, this routes us to the Sixth Regiment. Isn't that in the area of Supreme Headquarters?" Saltz asked.

"This could be good. Even if this guy proved to be a hoax, we would be near our original target, HQ," I said.

"Ah Sing wishes to know, 'Is there problem?'" Dit Swan asked.

"Dit Swan, tell him we doubt that this letter is authentic. This man says he is American, but we find him hard to believe. We think it's a Jap trap!" Hump said.

"Ah Sing say not to worry. He send guerrillas to protect. One tommy gun and seven rifle. Also, letter for each headquarters to give protection."

"What about our guns, Dit Swan?"

"Yes, the pistols be with you, when you meet American."

"How far to the American?" Hump asked.

"Long journey, many footsteps," Ko Shing said.

April 28, 1945—It sounds like a 200-mile walk. We wait for a couple of days for a letter to come from Woo Ping.

The Japs have been fighting with them and no one knows the results and which route is the safest. I certainly hope we don't travel the same route we had coming down here.

The Capt. told us tomorrow he would point out places on the map, where we could have American airplanes drop guns and other equipment that Hump has promised the American government would do, for helping us.

We gave them a set of maps and the one compass we had plus our leather gloves . . . Made trade of Carl's coveralls for a shirt with Ko Shing—now have two shirts and two pants, since cutting my flight suit in half.

Another gift this morning, handkerchief that 1000 single Japanese girls put a stitch in for the protection of the soldier who carries same. The fellow who carries this is never supposed to die, but lo and behold he is dead.

April 30, 1945—Can't hear out of my right ear at all and Hump's ear is running pretty bad. We received three pair of ivory chopsticks, each worth $1000 Jap money, from Ko Shing. Ear opened up for a short while and the future looks or rather sounds better, but jaw all swollen for some reason or other. Damn, I go from one thing to another.

May 3, 1945—May first being a holiday for these people and having to carry foodstuffs and work that day, today was declared the day of celebration. Duck, coffee, wood potatoes and flour, with fish and bamboo rolled inside. Not bad—not good.

Clever show and nearly everyone was called on to sing or do some act. We sang, "Working on the Railroad" and "Old MacDonald had a Farm" and received much applause. Several acts by Chinese, with four or five scenes, were very interesting. "The Jap Spy, The Chinese Buddha

Priests, The Dancing Girls," and all girl parts were played by Chinese fellows. A lad who is an excellent harmonica player rendered a few American tunes, much to our delight. It took me home for a while.

"Tonight we celebrate your good fortune, going home to America," Foo Yin announced. "Please do not forget your jungle comrades. We wish you safe journey."

"Thank you, Foo Yin," Hump said.

Ko Shing stood and addressed us. "Our wonderful friends. When home in America, please tell your government to help us win independence. We much like you. Eager to be free. This we cannot have when Japs and British force their life on Malayans. Most cruel fascists and imperialists come here and take our land and freedom. We will fight and die. This we do for our country. I hope to see you again one day."

Dit Swan reminded me to give the "Nine Points of Malayan Communist Party" to our government.

These Chinese had been wonderful! They had taken excellent care of us and done their best to make our stay comfortable. Despite the high cost and difficulty of obtaining food, we had eaten better than anywhere since landing, plus enjoyed coffee nearly every day.

It's like old friends parting and they asked we never forget them.

How could I ever forget?

Currency of the Third Regiment
Malayan People's Anti-Japanese Army
March 1944

"Drive the Japanese out of Malaya and Establish a Republic"

Two-Hundred-Mile Trek

May 7, 1945—0800 - We departed with eight guards, seven rifles and one tommy gun. Saltz not feeling well, malaria and upset stomach. Today, he is 25 years old. Hump and I have cramps and backdoor trots. Must be all the good food at the banquet. Despite our poor health we arrived at #23 camp at 1400.

Banquet and celebration tonight—wine, chicken, steak, chow mein and pickled papaya. Celebration because, "Hitler was killed in Berlin by bombs and Mussolini, along with many others, was captured." Wonderful news!

Next day, Saltz and Hump much better and I fell ill. Cramps, stomach pain, fever, and bones aching. Each day grew worse, adding dizzy spells and vomiting. I feared appendicitis. I lagged behind the rest, and Hump would keep checking to see if I was still on my feet. I would wave him on, knowing there was nothing he could do, as I struggled. Aside from my illness, this journey was much better than our last. The rain wasn't bad and the flooding and rivers had receded.

One early evening, many loud elephant calls began nearby. The noise was tremendous, as they trampled dense vegetation, crashing and ripping out trees or anything in their path. We stared at the dark without blinking, turning an ear to gauge the direction of their path. The Chinese laughed, but we had no desire to be in an elephant's path!

May 16, 1945—Departed by sampan at 1830, after almost sinking it at shore, and crossed Tasek Bera by torchlight. Seven rode in our sampan and the water line was a half-inch from the top. Several times we almost capsized and took in plenty of water. We had to be still in this long, narrow boat, and it caused terrible leg cramps and numbness. Never in my life have I seen such a dark, dark, dismal swamp. The picture "Swamp Water" didn't depict the terror we felt, and that was supposed to have been filmed in Okefenokee Swamp, Florida. Crocodile, snakes, large hairy spiders and dripping branches slapped at our faces, while a foul odor rose off the swamp. We were wet, cold, tired and hungry—two hours I hope never to experience again. We were even happy to be back at Woo Ping's camp.

"Welcome friends, happy to see you!" English Tom said as we entered camp.

Wet and covered head to foot in mud, we were in no mood for socials. Tom changed things with his next comment.

"Have you heard wonderful news? War over in Europe. Germany surrender, Hitler dead!"

I couldn't believe my ears. Hump, Saltz and I began hugging everyone. Hooting and hollering, we danced around until we collapsed on our bottoms. The guerrillas and women were wild with laughter. English Tom stayed his distance, leery of our hugging, I guess.

May 16, 1945—Here we were on the 16th finding out what everybody in the States had been drunk over for 10 days. Oh well! Our day will come in the not too distant future. I bet Peg's heart is aching now that all those boys are being released from the army and being sent home. Well, darling, I know it hurts. Many graces will follow, so be patient honey!

We sat down to our meal of rice and rice broth, compliments of Woo Ping. He said we would leave by sampan the next day, to cross Tasek Bera and continue our journey.

Visiting again with English Tom, Yung Han, Asui, Bartholomew, and other dear Chinese friends was wonderful. Despite the harsh life one must endure in the jungle, these people were a blessing. Of course this didn't include Woo Ping and loyal Communists.

We ran into the young lad who had helped give us our first meal in Malaya, one of the Chinese who had served us rice and tea before the Japs had interrupted us on the trail. He had visited Ralph Lindley in jail, but he couldn't tell us what became of Lindley. Funny to meet this boy after four months in the jungle.

Next day, a one-hour sampan ride and ten hours of walking brought us to our first Sakai village. We were greeted by a dozen men, women and children. The brown-skinned natives, clad only in loincloth, gathered around Hump, Saltz and me, to get a close look at their first Americans. We were on display. They felt our skin and hair, examined our eyes and measured our hands and feet in comparison to their smaller ones. They chattered and laughed as their curiosity led them to study our odd features.

The Sakai women walked around with bare breasts and I've never seen such huge things in my life. Out of proportion from nursing the children and hanging so low. It was hard not to stare at them and I was uneasy being so close to them.

Both men and women had cigarettes dangling from their lips. The old boys were characters, but I imagine they thought the same of us.

We received a goat as a present. It was slaughtered and served for our evening meal. I thought of Chicago—my home, clothes, food, everything I have available for my personal comfort and security. The Sakai's existence is the jungle, a loincloth, a blowgun and spear, and a *basha* on stilts. Malnutrition was very prevalent. But their kindness, friendship and love were remarkable.

I was told they serve a god. It must have been the same God I serve, because they lived by the teaching I received. They exemplified love as no one I had ever known. Thousands of miles from home, in the dark solid jungle, a people who have nothing else to give taught me a lesson in love. I could see that my daily prayers for safety, health and passage home were being answered in the form of Sakai and Chinese aid.

The following morning we woke to the chatter of five families, anxious to scrutinize us from head to toe. We received more gifts. Two fowl, a basket of rice, and many pineapples, which we ate with the balance of the goat for breakfast.

With the aid of the Sakai we blazed a trail north to the Bera River, through grasses and reeds over our heads to avoid a Jap hot area. Our trek left us weak and tired. We spent four and a half hours, inching our way by machete while gasping for air in the searing heat, drenched in sweat.

I had a pretty bad skin rash covering much of my body and this irritated it further. But I thought all I needed was a good bath, with soap, and a little sunshine on my skin. Actually, we had had no soap in over a month and the jungle's canopy leaves little opportunity for the sun's rays to penetrate. Once we hit the Sixth Regiment, I figured I'd get that sun.

At the Bera River, Hump, one Sakai and three guerrillas headed downriver by sampan, while the remainder of us waited for its return. Meanwhile, several crocodile slid into the water around us, preventing us from cooling off in the water or getting in some shut-eye. Three hours dragged, until the sampan returned to give us a fifty-minute ride to another Sakai village.

We learned that the old guy who had escorted us was the chief Sakai of the area, known to the people as "Father." As his guests, we accepted gifts of two chickens and a young goat and asked they be prepared for dinner.

Many women were present. One young woman wore only a scanty G-string. She was pretty, shapely, and well endowed. Nudity was natural for the Sakai, but it made me sort of uncomfortable. Saltz thought he had died and gone to heaven. Hump and I insisted he would be sleeping between us that night and to forget about heaven.

On day thirteen we arrived at a guard post to Camp Number 162 of the Sixth Regiment. The officers refused us admittance after reading our letters—used as our passport—and said guards would escort us in two days. Until now, we had been in camps reporting to Ah Sing and Woo Coo Shing at Third Regiment Headquarters. Now, we were dealing with the Communists of another regiment.

May 22, 1945—In two days, I was sicker than I had ever been in my life. Fever and chills had me shaking under three blankets, vomiting all solids or fluids, and painful cramps were joined by diarrhea. The escort showed, but I couldn't travel, so tomorrow we leave.

The little Chinese girl in this basha is a spoiled brat. She passes water and craps right on the table, chairs, floor or wherever she happens to be. She is constantly shoving something into her mouth and she whines all the time. If any of my children are like this, they had better look out!

Took plenty of quinine and started to feel better toward evening, still weak and stomach is upset. Many pains and my chest is hurting again from the injury received bailing out of the plane.

Married 2 years, 9 months today and have been with Peg not quite a year. What a deal. I certainly hope our future will not be the same. I love you, Redhead!

May 24, 1945—Feel a little better after sweating all night. Hump still has diarrhea—two weeks now— and a fever. Damn Malaya! Had our clothes mended again. Once we gathered them, we pulled out with four guerrillas. Our lead man, who spoke the only English, we called Fritz.

At 1730, we stopped at a farmhouse. Had two birds that a fellow just bagged with a shotgun, and rice—pretty good. The first meal I was able to hack in two days.

Started out to cross a railroad with three additional men, at 2100, crossing under a full moon. After walking another hour we arrived at a hut high atop a hill. Ate papaya, bananas, pineapples & sugar cane. No sleep all night with the mosquitoes. They ate us alive!

"Tell Fritz I can't leave this morning, I'm burning with fever," Hump said.

"How about the backdoor trots?" Saltz asked.

"Bad as ever—could it be any other way? Seems I got them for life!"

We started laughing and it felt good. For the past two weeks we hadn't shared in any laughter. Illness, rain, bloodthirsty mosquitoes, heat and humidity by day, then bone-chilling cold at night and always compounded by wet blankets and clothes. Such was the Malaya jungle.

"Saltz, how is it that you manage to stay healthy, except for your bouts with malaria?" Hump grumbled. "I mean what's the deal here, you got green blood or jungle lineage?"

"Don't know what to tell you boys, guess you're out of shape. If it's too much for you, maybe you shouldn't have come to Malaya."

The laughter put aside the hardship and poor spirit we acquired, drawing us closer. The past four months we tired of each other, having been too close for too long and living three degrees off the equator in this hot miserable jungle.

We didn't talk about what we feared most—death. Some days you were ready to die, to be done with the agony. But we kept fighting . . . that will to survive . . . hope for tomorrow . . . an end to the war. Maybe— escape from Malaya and its jungle.

Neither Hump nor Saltz had a wife or steady girl back home. Saltz had a sister, Mary, in Washington, D.C., and Hump his parents in Postville, Iowa, a brother stationed in England, and one sister. I had Peggy, Danny and Peggy Anne. Plus, my folks, a sister Lorraine and two brothers, Bob and Don. Peggy and the little ones were my hope and desire to live and make it back.

May 26, 1945—Walked five hours today, but on the trail seven or more. Hump has fallen heir to a half-dozen blisters on each foot, caused by wearing this solid rubber shoe issued by the Communists. Barefoot proved better in the jungle. Before our boots wore out, our feet were rotting from moisture and bacteria, or some foot fungus. It was growing in our boots and then on our feet. No wonder these people go barefoot or wear an open shoe.

We stumbled onto a water hole, with what appeared to be a prehistoric monster encamped in it. He took off hell bent for election when he heard us. He was huge— about six feet long, one and half feet high and had four large thorny legs. Quite a sight. Naturally, we expected to see another jump out and attack us on every turn. No one was too anxious to take the lead after that little event. But after an hour we settled down.

We stayed put on account of Hump's blisters. They're

pretty sore and we soaked them all day, with hopes of leaving tomorrow. I hope we can, because my fever is back and there's no telling what may develop. Our quinine supply is at rock bottom. Rice is the only food.
Two more bowls of rice and ten hours on the trail. Tough on Hump's feet. Walked parallel to a railroad track and the Chinese constantly told us to not to talk on account of the Japs. One lad held a hand grenade for two hours. We never saw a thing, but the anxiety kept us charged.
Received word at a Chinese kampong that the Japs are near. Fritz headed us up the side of a hill to an old Sakai hut. Rice, sugar cane and rest. Boys said I talked all night in my sleep. Malaya has got me!

Headquarters was three more days away. The Japs were after the Sixth Regiment—the report was that thousands of Japs were scouring the jungle to trap and wipe out the guerrillas. The guerrilla leaders had abandoned headquarters and were moving fast through the jungle, stopping only a few hours at outposts and abandoning camps as they moved deeper into the hilly region. We were to head west to the hills for a rendezvous.

Hump's feet were a little better, but I didn't know if he could stand up to more trekking and climbing.

My skin rash had spread, up the inside of both arms, stomach, waist and thighs, but stopped short of the family jewels, and for this I was grateful.

We left at noon, climbing some hills in country that was the most beautiful we had seen, but would have looked better from a sedan seat. We walked along a crystal-clear river, really a majestic sight. Arriving at a farmhouse, we held up, waiting for information on the Japs' location.

It was a touchy position, because the Japs had been attacking these people for the past two days. We were taking plenty of chances on our little walk, crossing the Karak motor road and a rubber estate. We stopped two miles west of the road, putting us four miles from Karak. The whole area was under surveillance. The bags were packed, but we stayed the night.

Miserable night's sleep, with the damn mosquitoes and body ticks burrowing into our skin. In Malaya, everyone was starving except the insects.

The four men who escorted us from Camp Number 162 were on constant guard and ready to move. All day long people were coming to the farmhouse, some carrying grenades.

The word finally came: "The Japs are coming."

We acted quickly, moving upriver and into the hills.

After an hour, we came to another farm at the edge of the jungle.

"We wait here," Fritz told us, not offering any information. We were happy to rest, after the fast pace and load we carried. The gear was a second skin, always at your side or on your back, crucial to our survival.

"Hump, how are the feet?" I asked. "You're limping again."

"They're in pretty good shape, but I hope we don't do any running. I don't think I could bear much, even with the Japs chasing my tail."

"I'll talk to Fritz. Let's see if we can find a hiding place and get you some rest."

In the next breath, twenty yards away, the jungle bushes burst open and a string of soldiers rushed at us. Hump, Saltz and I froze a moment, surprised by the number of men and their quick entrance. We grabbed our guns, but there was no time to escape. Fritz took a step toward them, raising his tommy gun. Hump, Saltz and I pointed our .45s as troops surrounded us.

Humphrey, Duffy & Saltzman – Malayan jungle.
Note the leech bites on the exposed flesh of Duffy's foot
and Saltzman's legs revealing a sample of the open sores
covering their bodies from the dreaded jungle leeches.

Sixth Regiment Headquarters

Fritz lowered his tommy gun. The uniformed men were Juju-Tui—Communist Chinese— our boys.

"Oh, I thought it was over!" I said.

"It would have been!" Hump said.

We breathed a sigh of relief. Fritz expected their arrival, but as usual we weren't told a thing. Damn Communists!

Twenty-five guerrillas surrounded us. They were members of the Sixth Regiment Headquarters detachment and their officers

"Major Humphrey, Lieutenant Duffy, Lieutenant Saltzman, introduce you Ma-Tin, First Captain Political Leader and Chen Ping, Second Captain Propaganda," Fritz said. They gave a raised-fist salute and we returned the honor with ours.

One Chinese lad we mistook as English. He

certainly appeared English in dress and manner. He wore a derby—a stiff felt hat with a round crown and a narrow curved brim—and leaned on a hand-carved Malaccan cane. His dress included a white short-sleeve button-down shirt, dark pants and wire-rim spectacles. It was a peculiar sight for the jungle.

"What have we here?" Saltz mumbled. "I say, is this chap primped for 'afternoon tea'?" Hump and I bit our lips. Saltz's sense of humor often lacked tact. He wasn't a bit uneasy making cracks about people when they were within earshot.

"Hello—I am Cheng Swee Kim, interpreter for the Sixth Regiment. It is a pleasure to meet you." The lad spoke excellent English.

"Thank you! We have looked forward to this day for many months," Hump said.

"We will have to save our visiting for later. Ma-Tin and Chen Ping wish to leave immediately, for the Japanese troops are not far behind. The murderers have been terrorizing farmers and their families as they chase our regiment."

"We're ready," Hump said.

Before we departed, more guerrillas arrived, bringing the count in our party to nearly fifty. I felt pretty secure with such a force. The troops were outfitted with rifles, tommy guns, English bren guns, shotguns, handguns and grenades, which many carried in their hands.

We continued upriver, wading thigh deep, for the next hour. The trip was orderly and little was said, except for the captains' periodic orders. Toward nightfall we left the river and scaled a hill. The three of us puffed our way to the top, dripping in sweat. Here we made camp.

Our features and skin color fascinated the Chinese. I imagine most were seeing their first Americans. Again, it was Hump who caught the most attention with his lean six-foot frame and curly dark hair. Saltz didn't attract much, nor I except for my blue eyes. They were amazed by how dripping wet we got when we perspired. Their bodies were accustomed to the climate and although they did sweat, it was nothing compared to the faucets we turned on.

Rice and coffee were served for dinner. With Cheng translating, the chiefs opened up the discussion. "How was the journey from Third Regiment Head-quarters, were there any problems with the Japs?" Ma-Tin asked.

"No—no problem with Japs, just our health," Hump said. He had another fever. It showed in his voice. "It took twenty-three days, but we were well cared for."

"How is your health now?" Cheng asked.

"We've been holding up pretty good. The malaria and backdoor trots have been difficult and Duff's intestine or stomach pain has given him a bad time."

"Backdoor trots?" Cheng asked. We burst into laughter, while the Chinese smiled and waited for an explanation.

"I'm sorry, I mean watery stools, bowels." Saltz and I couldn't stop laughing. The more Hump said, the worse we got.

"Oh, I understand!" Cheng laughed and trans-lated Hump's explanation. Before Cheng had finished,

Ma-Tin, Chen Ping and everyone within earshot broke out in laughter.

"Do you need any quinine for the malaria?" Cheng asked.

"Yes, we do."

"Do you have a fever?"

"Yes."

Cheng spoke to the captains, and Hump was led away to be cared for by two of the guerrillas.

"Thank you, Cheng. We appreciate your kindness," I said. Cheng bowed his head and smiled.

"We are sorry about your comrade who died at Second Regiment. Which of you was with him?"

"It was me," I said. The memory was less painful. Many nights I faced awful nightmares, but they eased with time.

"You are Duffy?" Cheng asked.

"Yes, Bill Duffy."

"And you are Saltman?"

"Saltzman, Cliff Saltzman."

"Forgive me."

"That's okay."

"Chen Ping wishes to know where you are from?" Cheng asked.

"I am from Washington, D.C.," Saltz said. "Don Humphrey is from Postville, Iowa, and Duff is from Chicago, Illinois."

"Did you know one another before the war?" Ma-Tin asked.

"No, we met after enlisting in the Army Air Corps," Saltz said.

"Ma-Tin, does the Sixth Regiment have a radio?"

Saltz cut through the small talk and got to the point of our journey to the Sixth Regiment.

"No, there is no radio. We communicate by runner. It is quite effective, considering the ground they cover."

"Yes, we are familiar with your messengers. But we were hoping to radio the Allies—South East Asia Command—to have a submarine pick us up," Saltz said.

"Ma-Tin, do any of your camps have a radio?" I asked.

"Central Military Headquarters has that information."

"Are we going to Central Headquarters?"

"No. You are not permitted. Few are admitted to this camp, except high-ranking officers."

"Ma-Tin and Chen Ping, are they permitted?" I asked.

"Yes—at times they attend conferences with the Central Committee."

"Can they send word and request a radio transmission be sent to South East Asia Command?"

"Ma-Tin will consider your request. But for now we have to deal with the Japs. They are hunting us like animals in hope of wiping out our regiment."

"What can you tell us about this American, J. Jack Bussey?" I asked.

"Ma-Tin says we will talk about him another time. Right now he wishes to know what you think of the Chinese Communist in Malaya."

Here we go again with our thoughts on Communism! I would love to tell these bastards how I hate

Communism—its lies, deception, and propaganda. This country is in trouble. The Japs have invaded, the British have fled, and the Communists hope to take over when the Japs are defeated. God help this country!

Sleep was impossible. Besides mosquitoes and body ticks we had gas bombs and snoring, then before daylight the rain began. My blanket was soaked, passing the wetness to my clothes and sending a terrible chill to my joints and bones. I lay awake in a fetal position, shivering.

Little was said at breakfast while we sat wrapped in wet blankets eating cold rice.

Despite the conditions, there was beautiful music playing as the rain danced with the leaves. At the moment I was at peace . . . able to admire the jungle's splendor, with its abundant plant life, vines and trees taking root and seeking nourishment from the sun and rain. When I cleared my head of thoughts of our difficulties and indulged in the mystery of life and its gifts, I could see the hand of God. Nature with its magnificence and beauty has always been a powerful reminder for me.

It hit me again, how these people had lived in the jungle for over three years . . . I wondered who they were . . . where they were from . . . what their lives were like before the war . . . my eyes scanned the troops while they squatted and ate rice, as the rain drenched their clothes and chilled their bodies.

The Chinese have a unique ability to squat rather than sit, during a conversation or meal. I couldn't adapt. It usually led to muscle cramps as the circulation in my legs quit. But I could see how it came in handy in a wet jungle to keep your bottom high and dry.

"Cheng, where are we headed today?" Hump asked.

"We will continue west, higher in the hills. The Japs are searching the entire region and it is certain they will make their way along the river, and north of it, as they come this way."

We departed at 0630 in a steady rain. We traveled on a wild animal's path that closed in on us in the first hour. We blazed through a wall of jungle growth, only to accept defeat after thirty minutes and head back down to the river we had left the day before. It was a terrible risk to retrace our steps and head toward the Japs, but our escape was blocked—we had to find another way.

Growth on both sides of the river grew to the water's edge, forcing us to wade. It was calf deep, but its current was strong. Climbing upriver, we slipped on algae, roots and rocks. We climbed over and under countless tree trunks and received hundreds of paperlike cuts from an innocent-looking reed or grass, which left a painful sting.

The trek lasted six hours and we didn't make a mile. The site of our camp was not far from the water and a bath refreshed my bruised body.

I lay in the river holding onto a tree root, while the fast water caressed my aching muscles. My naked body looked gaunt. I was still about sixty pounds light since my illness, leaving me weighing less than ninety pounds. The rash was worse. Painful sores dotted my body. It reminded me of poison ivy. Every few days it blistered, drained, and blistered again. Amazing how much disease and illness our bodies withstood.

Our skin was gray. I could distinguish it in Hump and Saltz and they assured me mine was gray too. It lacked sun. Seldom did the jungle allow more than a flicker of the sun's rays to pass through its canopy and touch its floor. I recalled hearing about coal miners back home in the States, whose skin took on a gray color because they worked underground during the day and their skin didn't get enough sunlight.

I also lacked energy and strength, which I believe the sun could have helped provide. God knows the rice diet didn't fulfill the body's craving. But we were alive!

The second evening—after rice and tea—Hump opened a discussion with the two captains and Cheng translated.

"Ma-Tin, please tell us about J. Jack Bussey."

"Bussey is an American. He is part of the First Detachment who parachuted from a *Liberator*, last December. Three Chinese accompany him. He was sent to contact the Anti-Jap Army to gather information on the Japs and locate an Englishman hiding in the jungle. We have asked him to join our party, but he refuses."

"Where is Bussey?" Hump asked.

"He is fifteen days' journey from us."

"He wrote us this letter, saying that he can radio for help and arrange an escape by submarine." Hump showed the letter.

"Yes, we have seen this letter. Central Headquarters recommends not contacting this Bussey. We do not believe this man is concerned with military affairs.

You should wait for the Second Detachment being sent by South East Asia Command. We believe they have already landed in Malaya, but not at their designated site."

"How will you find the Second Detachment?" Hump asked.

"They will contact the Anti-Jap Army and we will receive this information by messenger. This detachment will do more for you."

It certainly looked like we would be here for some time. We wrote two letters: one to Bussey and the other to Central Headquarters. We enclosed our names and serial numbers and these people said headquarters would forward them to South East Asia Command. I hoped so, because that certainly would relieve Peggy's mind and also my folks'—thank God!

Next morning, our troops continued upriver, walking an hour before breakfast. We came to a stream that fed into the river. We followed upstream—walking in the water forty minutes—to a place the captains decided to build a temporary camp. Here we would stay until we got information the Japs had quit the search.

I spent several days with Cheng, sharing thoughts and opinions on a wide range of topics. Cheng gave me a political science book by W.B. Curry, *The Case for Federal Union*. I read most of the day and he and I engaged in discussion that evening.

"Cheng, I'm surprised you have this book!"

"I favor a democratic government, such as the United States, Bill. I'm afraid this is not true of my comrades. We may both believe in a free Malaya, but I am concerned that the motive of the Communists is selfish and does not include all Malayans."

"I thought you were a Communist," I said.

"No—I prefer the British over the Communist. Of course, I ask you keep this to yourself."

"It's difficult to believe you. If you're not a Communist, why are you working with the Sixth Regiment?"

"It is a long story, but the short of it is, I prefer life over death! If I stayed in Kuala Lumpur, I would be dead. My uncle is a high-ranking Communist officer and I would be singled out because we are related. It was a matter of time before the Japs grabbed me and put my head on display or forced me to serve in their military against my people. So I used my uncle to gain position with the guerrillas. Not many of the guerrillas can speak English, which makes me valuable. I learned in school as a young boy."

"Missionary school?" I asked.

"Yes, how did you know?"

"I met a lad who is with the Second Regiment, who was schooled in Malacca."

"My father is a wealthy businessman in Singapore. He made sure I learned English. He believes an advantage exists, with such a tool. I believe it has kept me alive and offers a valuable position with the guerrillas."

"Yes, Ma-Tin and Chen Ping appear to treat you well."

"They treat me fair. I am not called on for labor or transporting supplies and this makes life better."

"Your home is Kuala Lumpur?"

"Yes, I live with my mother, sister and grandfather. Father makes his home in Singapore, though he frequently comes home."

"Is your family safe, with the Jap occupation?"

"I believe my mother, sister and grandfather are healthy, but we never heard from my father after the Japs took Singapore. I retreated to the jungle in May 1942. Prior to that I heard many stories of what took place in Singapore and the Peninsula."

"What happened in Singapore, Cheng?"

"The British surrendered to the Japs and all were imprisoned at Changi. Reports say they are starving to death. After the surrender, the Japs placed all the Chinese under arrest, to weed out people they believed would be a problem. Door to door, soldiers with bayonets and rifles kicked in doors and gathered every man, woman and child by the thousands, leading them to large open areas throughout Singapore. There was no food, water, or shade provided.

"They were ordered to remain standing like cattle or required to squat without getting up while their legs cramped. If they spoke out they were kicked, slapped and beaten. People were not allowed to use latrines, they were told to let it out where they stood. Forced into humiliation—men, women and children relieved themselves in front of one another. Afterward, officers would come by and see the feces and demand the identity of the person, then instruct their soldiers to kick and beat them for their indecency.

"Night came and sleep was impossible. There was not enough room for people to lie down, and there was urine and feces everywhere. They suffered from exposure in the cold of night and millions of mosquitoes came down on them.

"Without food or water and standing under the

scorching sun, hundreds of men, women, and children—including infants and the elderly—suffered and died of sunstroke and thirst. This continued for three and four days.

"Chinese informers, wearing hoods on their heads, singled out and identified Communists or anyone thought to be trouble. Thousands of people were tortured, but later found innocent. So they were released with a strict warning of the penalty awaiting them, should they not cooperate.

"Chinese who were thought to be guilty faced a firing squad, were bayoneted, or beheaded. The dead lay everywhere, corpses rotting among the living. Rats fed on the dead and half-living.

"Women and young girls whose looks appealed to the Japs were loaded into lorries and driven away, never to be seen again. It is suspected they were used to satisfy the sexual appetites of the Jap officers and then discarded and repeatedly raped by the troops and forced into prostitution.

"In the *kampongs* of the peninsula, countless women and girls were raped. Many were left dead or dying after the Jap attackers had had their fill with their bodies. The Japs' laughter could be heard, while screams and wailing echoed through the night. Tears rain hard on Malaya for her women!

"In Kuala Lumpur, the Japs cut off the heads of Chinese and display them on the end of a pole, the wall of a bridge, maybe in the local market.

"I shall never forget my neighbor's execution. He was accused of stealing food. We knew he had no money and was trying to feed his family, but to speak out on his behalf would mean death for us too.

"An officer turned his sword over to a Jap sentry and gave the command. A swift blow sliced through the man's neck and his head fell to the street. It rolled and spun briefly, then stopped where the face and open eyes looked up at me. The body crumbled and fell, and blood poured from the hole on its shoulders. I vomited on myself and the Jap soldiers laughed at me. The head was displayed for days."

Recounting the stories awakened Cheng's pain and agony. He wiped tears from his cheeks and rubbed them on his pant leg.

The Japs' atrocities were cruel and evil. The day would come when they would feel the Allies' sword fall on them!

Cheng continued. "Japs keep order by threatening to torture people. The stories are well known and terrify everyone. The investigation of a suspect to crime starts with torture. The Jap usually begins by kicking, slapping and boxing the person's face. Pliers are used to rip off their fingernails and toenails. They whip your bare body, tearing the flesh and making it bleed. Prisoners will hang for hours upside down or balancing on just their toes. Hands and feet are burned till charred. The suspect will have a hose stuck in his mouth, while gallons of water will be pumped into his body. Then they jump on the bloated stomach till the water and blood run from the eyes, nose, mouth, ears, and other openings. The hose may instead be stuck in the rectum, and then the person is filled with boiling water. In all, torture prolongs the victim's life, giving the Jap great satisfaction. Those who die quick are the most fortunate."

Nearby, a commotion interrupted Cheng's story. We joined Hump, Saltz, and a half dozen of our boys.

The Chinese had caught a ten-foot snake in camp. It was three inches in diameter and they killed it by strangulation. They cut into it and there was a four and half foot snake inside its stomach. It had chewed the hell out of it, before swallowing it whole. We had the big snake with our evening meal and a more tasty meat has not passed my palate.

June 9, 1945—Sick all day. Terrible cramps and pains in abdomen. Appendicitis still worries me. Rest and wait. Chen Ping and Cheng came back today and they brought a "basketball and violin." Imagine the surprise. The captain serenaded us and he was pretty good.

I wrapped my arms around the basketball and pulled it to my stomach. The feel of the dimples on the ball passed through my fingers and the sensation from rolling and flipping it in my hands delighted and energized my body. I set up the ball—one hand on the bottom and the other on top—adjusting the fingers for the proper feel to take a shot. I planted my feet and balanced my body to the stance I used back home, to execute my fade-away jump shot. I released the ball, confident its arch and path were correct from the feel passing through my fingers and hands.

Fifteen feet away stood Hump, with his arms formed as a hoop to receive my shot, while I commented: "Yes, folks, Duffy takes his fade-away jump shot from fifteen feet out and swishes it with no time on the clock, putting his team ahead and winning the game!"

The second day Hump, Saltz and I—with the aid of Cheng and a group of guerrillas—set up a playing area for a basketball court. We constructed it using a tree branch for the pole and a vine looped into a hoop. We made up a game called "jungle ball," passing, running, colliding, pushing and shooting with two teams of four players.

After a few days the ball popped, which was fine . . . we realized that we hadn't the physical strength after all. But the basketball had lifted our spirits and returned some life to our deprived and depleted bodies. Like boys on a playground, we were filled with joy, laughter and friendship at our jungle hideout.

Forgot to mention that our boys in the 3rd Regiment attacked the town of Segamat. Other towns were attacked at the same time and many police joined forces with these people. They confiscated plenty of guns.

Cheng—our interpreter and the most entertaining Chinese fellow we have so far contacted—gave us a lot of newspapers written in English, which were published by the Anti-Jap Army. They told of the collapse of Germany and about Hitler's, Goebbel's (Hitler's buddy—the Nazi propaganda minister), Mussolini's and many other deaths. He also translated Chinese papers and brought us up to date on the war.

This lad has certainly gone out of his way to please us and he is a constant source of information. He hasn't been influenced too much by his Communist environment and has a wonderful sense of humor. The captains realize we enjoy his company and instead of transferring him to the other camp—where the paper section is—they let him remain here. Good deal! He came from a rather wealthy family and did nothing except go to the movies four or five times a day, prior to the Jap occupation. This was his means to pick up and learn about the United States and our way of life.

Life in this camp isn't bad, except for the various forms of recurring illnesses I have and the fact that Cheng constantly tells me my hair is falling out!

"The Second Detachment has landed and contacted Central Headquarters," Chen Ping informed us.

"Great! Where are they located?" Hump asked.

"Fourteen days' march."

"When did they arrive?"

"They parachuted in February." We couldn't believe our ears. It was June 11 and they're just receiving the news.

"How many landed?" I asked.

"Nine. Four Englishmen, two Australians, two Chinese and one Malay. They were dispatched from South East Asia Command."

Hump, Saltz and I were delighted by the news. Maybe now we could get moving to bring about our long-awaited departure. But our wish died quickly. The Japs continued the pressure, hitting small bands of guerrillas and holding public executions. Farmers were being tortured into providing the whereabouts of Communist hideouts; the Japs set fire to their homes and bayoneted or shot them point blank in the head.

Another bad malaria spell and terrific stomach pain put me down for five days. Two Chinese doctors handled my case and said it was not appendicitis. I drank several cups of witches' broth and was told I would pass the bad blood with my excretion. Two days passed and no blood and the doctors began to wonder. Sure would like to have had a western doctor diagnose my case.

Hump and I had a debate on when the war would end. "Duff, I bet the Japs will be licked and the war will end by June 20."

"How's that, Hump?"

"Heck, the Americans are transferring twenty-four thousand bombers and twelve thousand fighters to the Far East. The Japs can't last much longer."

"You're rather optimistic, Major Humphrey. Are you willing to wager?"

"Absolutely!"

"How much, Hump? It's your call. I want you to set your own level of despair."

"Three hundred American dollars."

"It's a deal. Let's shake on it. Saltz and Cheng, you're witnesses."

"This is exciting!" Cheng said.

The closer to June 20, the more optimistic Hump became. "The Japs can't last much longer." June 19 arrived and Hump said, "Well, the war will be over tomorrow."

"Let's get our bags packed, so we're ready to move into the nearest town," I suggested.

June 20, 1945—The war is over today! Hump hasn't heard a Nip airplane all day and he was sweating it out. Earned myself $300, but would rather have seen an end to this damn war.

Saltz is in excellent health, as always, and Hump is back to normal. I'm feeling much better and hope there is some news soon.

Cheng still a great help to us and he has become an

intimate friend. His thoughts and words are so different from the party's ideas. Of course his education is the main factor for this contrast. Chen Ping is a rabid preacher of Communism and rarely takes a break from filling our heads with propaganda. Each night he indulges in his "nocturnal pollutions" and isn't worth a damn the next day.

The Jap situation continues to get worse. It appears the Japs captured more Communist guerrillas and tortured them to obtain the Sixth Regiment's current location. We are playing cat and mouse.

I prayed.

We evacuated camp and hurried to put some ground between the Japs and us, before losing daylight. The last hour was a disaster. Many of us were separated from the company, losing the trail in the dark. I was with Saltz and four guerrillas. One spoke just a bit of English.

These characters didn't know where we were. We pushed on and it grew darker. Vegetation closed in, pressing against us from all sides. Saltz and I fell three and four times.

"That's it, we stop here!" I yelled.

"Agreed. This is crazy." Saltz echoed. "We'll get killed romping around in the dark. We'll either fall off a ledge, down a hill, or walk smack into the Japs."

You could make out silhouettes of each other within four feet and faces within a foot. I asked the Chinese, "Do you have fire, flint?" I used my finger as a flint, striking it against the palm.

"No fire. No fire," responded our friend.

"Saltz, we're going to have to stay here tonight,

unless someone comes looking for us. We can't move in this darkness."

"I know. As much as I hate to sit here all night, I'm less fond of continuing."

"Let's take the machetes and clear an area to sit. It will give us a cushion to sleep on too," I said.

The Chinese followed our lead, slashing at the vegetation and presenting a clearing to house the six of us. Within an hour the moon rose and cast meager light through the trees on our site.

I turned to the boy with broken English and said, "Food, do you have food? Ask your friends, 'Do you have food?'"

"No food."

"Saltz, you got any food?"

"I got a couple pieces of sugar cane."

"And I got a chunk of sweet potato. Okay, we have dinner."

Five months of food shortage prepared us for these types of meals. In fact, when we came across a full meal and loaded our stomachs, we paid dearly with diarrhea and terrible stomach cramps. The body went into a fit. It reacted to a diet of food one day and no food the next twelve.

I cut the sweet potato into six pieces and passed them. Its sweet flavor lingered after I had rolled it around in my mouth and swallowed it. Saltz divided the sugar cane and we washed it down with the water Saltz and I carried in our canteens.

"The mosquitoes and bugs are terrible. They're all over me," I said.

"Yeah, this is murder. This will be a long night."

Digging into our packs, we covered our bodies with garments to protect our skin. We were always at a disadvantage. Morning meant new welts, bites, and swelling. Sun-up couldn't come soon enough. The battle robbed our sleep, and we cursed the night.

When mosquitos come down on you in the jungle, the torment they bring can lead to crazy thoughts of suicide and death. You wish to end the agony. Their constant humming, which seems to be just inside your ear, provokes a frantic and constant wave of the hand or slap at your head.

As the mosquitos lead you to insanity, there are also attacking swarms of biting midges—gnat-like flies that bite and bring about a nettlelike itch. Their little black bodies fly inches from your face every daylight hour, but they bite most viciously in the early hours before dawn.

At first light we moved out, the only true protection from mosquitos, bugs and other insects.

Within thirty minutes we met two more sections of lost men and the main body of the Sixth Regiment. Every man had suffered that night. Red welts on eyelids, lips, and cheeks distorted our faces. The swelling was so bad it was difficult to recognize some of the men.

After a bowl of hot rice, we began another tough day of climbing hills, descending only to climb another. The heat and humidity caused many of our boys to collapse, and spring water was difficult to find.

Each Regiment—Second, Third and Sixth—located itself with their backs to the hills and low mountains, so a retreat would take them upward to the thickest and most dense jungle. We found a position that afforded a broad overall view or perspective point, every direction revealed tree-clad hills. Peak after peak, ridge after ridge, no clearings of any sort. This was the most difficult jungle to penetrate, but tromping waist deep in swamp, bog, and mud tired and drained me just as much.

Pulling ourselves up the steep hills against sheets of rain beat our bodies and spirits. Climbing was impossible and we constantly slipped and fell. By nightfall we had terrible cuts, scratches and injuries in our attempt to penetrate the dense foliage. There was no camp on this journey, only the shelter of trees and bushes, but this didn't prevent insects from eating us alive.

Soaked and cold, we had no options. Going to bed soaking wet—in pouring rain—is perhaps the most miserable experience of my jungle life and it happened too often. As each experience occurred and I was forced to face it, it became the worst I could remember. Day by day, my struggle for health and strength was the most pressing battle I faced.

Days led into weeks. We moved almost daily during our escape with the Sixth Regiment. There was a constant fear the Japs would meet up with us. Finally, the word came.

"What's happening, Cheng?" I asked.

"The Japs have moved more troops into Bentong. You leave tomorrow night with Lao Woo—Number 2 Captain—head north and cross the Bentong road," Cheng said.

"Are you going, Cheng?"

"No, I must stay with the Sixth Regiment."

"Where is the regiment headed?"

"This you will not know. It is safer for the guerrillas, should you be captured."

"Where are we headed?"

"They will tell you in due time. But off the record, where did you want to go?"

"Thanks, Cheng!"

"Bill, I will miss you."

"I will miss you too, Cheng."

"Bill, what will you do when you get home? How will you live your life?"

"That's a million miles from here, Cheng. It's hard to think a lifetime, when each day is a question of life and death. We're not home yet."

"You will be, though. You have a family waiting."

"Yes, that beautiful redhead. Now there's a lifetime, Cheng! I'm going to make love to Peggy for the rest of my life."

"You won't last. You can't make it five months in the jungle."

I appreciated Cheng's humor and ability to make me laugh. His presence during the four weeks we spent with the Sixth Regiment was a blessing.

"What will you do when you get home, Cheng?"

"Go to the movies! I miss the movies."

We both laughed. But he turned serious and said, "I am concerned about how I will be received after spending three years with the Communists. Will I be frowned upon? Will I be offered a job, when they learn I worked with the Chinese Communists? I imagine I will be whispered about. And how will the government officials look upon me? These and other questions I have to face, when I return home!"

"Cheng, many of your people living with the Communists do so just to survive! Like you, they have fled the Japs and God knows they aren't Communists. In war, who we are is challenged; we make do with that which keeps us alive. I despise how they exploit the people of Malaya. They take young boys, still fresh and impressionable, and feed them propaganda until they reach in and steal their hearts. They mold them into extremists like themselves. These men are evil, but you aren't like them . . . you can go home and be proud that you served Malaya!"

"Bill—thank you for your kind words. Your friendship has touched my heart and there it will always remain. It is an honor to be your friend!"

"The honor is mine, Cheng! Thank you for making our time together pleasant. I would like us to write letters to one another and perhaps some day you will come to the United States or Peggy and I will come to Malaya."

"Yes, someday soon! I would like that."

"What will the Communists do when the war ends?"

"They will fight the British if an agreement for a free Malaya is not reached. They will require recognition as a legal party and spokesmen for the people. They plan to stockpile weapons, ammunition and supplies for the next war. They have laid the groundwork for an effective network of Communist guerrilla camps throughout Malaya, as you have witnessed. I believe this will be a major problem for the British and Malaya. The Communists hate the Japs, but they lie in wait for their true enemy, the British."

"I pray it won't come to that, Cheng. Your country and people have suffered enough bloodshed."

"I will not follow the Communists or support their politics. I believe the people of Malaya are on the road to independence and it will come in time."

"I hope you're right. Peaceful solution, with diplomacy. Please, be careful and get rid of that ridiculous derby hat and cane."

"Never!"

"I'll miss you, my friend."

"I'll miss you too, Bill."

The Malayan Jungle

British Second Detachment

Lao Woo and fifteen guerrillas led us north east toward Bentong. During a break, Lao Woo disclosed our destination, "Second Detachment and the British." It lightened my step to think we were headed for pay dirt.

Lao Woo was another who hated the British and white men, but he treated us fairly. Most of these boys saw us as an avenue to guns and supplies from our government and treated us with favor.

By late afternoon, we reached the motor road between Bentong and Karak. Lao Woo posted men on their bellies every twenty feet along the road. Using his rifle as a signal, he raised and pointed it at the other side. One man on either side of him sprang to his feet, hightailed across, and flopped on his belly in the grass at the road's edge. This continued two at a time until everyone had crossed, and we pushed deeper into the jungle.

Lao Woo proved to be one of the more organized and capable Communist leaders, using common sense and finesse in dangerous situations to avoid the enemy. He demanded his men follow his orders to the letter. I believe his skills kept us alive.

"These hills are murder!" Saltz moaned. As usual our bodies and clothes were drenched in sweat. We consumed more energy than we received in food and water, resulting in dehydration, cramps and fatigue.

In this heat and humidity, it always felt as if someone were standing on my chest. I couldn't breathe. For a time I was concerned about lung damage—from inhaling the burning fuel vapors of our airplane—or the chest injury when I slammed into the wheel mechanism. Maybe both! Regardless, the tropical air was terrible to breathe.

"Rain, rain, rain!" Hump cried. "How can this place have so much rain?"

"Remember what Cheng said?" I asked. "*There are two seasons in Malaya, rain and more rain. Winter monsoons from the North and summer monsoons from the South.*"

It doesn't just rain in Malaya—it's a constant downpour. We shared a faint laugh, huddled under a tree, hoping for a break. After an hour with no relief, Lao Woo ordered the group to push on in the pouring rain.

I took one step off the backside of a hill, slipped in the rain-soaked mud and fell on my rump. My fall didn't end until I reached the bottom and was tangled in the underbrush. I was already sopping wet. Now I was covered head to toe in mud.

"Duff, you okay?" Hump called. I lay in a heap at the bottom of the hill.

"I think so. Watch your step, it's slick. You're likely to loose your footing!" I had barely spoken when Saltz fell.

"Yipes, I'm down . . . I can't stop!" Saltz yelled, tumbling down the path I had created moments before.

"Don't worry, Saltz, you'll stop at the bottom!" I burst into laughter. Saltz lay at my feet and looked like something out of the swamp.

"Saltz, I didn't recognize you! Did you have a makeover—or a mud bath?"

"Oh, and aren't you the pretty one! I couldn't tell the front from the back of you, until you opened your mouth!"

I laughed so hard my chest hurt. I hadn't felt this good since we landed in Malaya. I looked up at Hump, and coaxed him to take his first step.

"Hump, I'll forget the money you owe me if you last three steps!"

"It's a deal! Three steps coming up, Duff."

He took one step, overcompensated a backward tilt and fell forward. He slid on his stomach, with arms out front splashing mud in his face, until he hit bottom. He piled into Saltz and me, and we lay there laughing, waiting for the Chinese to take the plunge.

The guerrillas—aware of the outcome—each sat down and took the ride on their tail ends. We had dealt with muddy paths and swampy trails each trek in our journey, but the laughter from the slipping and sliding that day lifted our spirits.

It was short-lived.

"Leeches!" Hump yelled.

We saw the monsters wiggling their way toward us. The ground was covered with them. It was impossible to walk without picking up five or six with each step of our bare feet. We couldn't stop and it made little sense to turn back, so we did our best to tie our pant bottoms with vines to keep them from crawling under our clothes. Regardless, they made their way in. We fought to keep our footing while climbing and descending hill after hill.

When I imagined the jungle, before Malaya, I never pictured dense hills and low mountains added to the already dreadful conditions. The journey beat us badly, dropping us to our knees. After every few minutes of climbing, we were forced to stop to catch our breath.

Five miles south of our location, there was a motor road traveling east and west, parallel to us. If we walked that road, it would cut days off our trip. But it was either the Japs or the jungle. That made our choice easy, but still agonizing. We lost either way!

June 28, 1945—Miserable night sleep, plenty of rain. I calculated how far we will have walked when we reach the Second Detachment—585 miles—oh, my aching back or rather feet.

Up at 0600 and depart at 0700—Leeches is all I can say for this leg of our trip. Saltz must have had over 100 bites. After seven brutal hours, we arrived at a farmhouse with many farmers and guerrillas. These people all seem to be working together. With the treatment and suffering the Japs have put on these people, they have made enemies of all.

After some time, a letter was handed to us from J. Jack Bussey in answer to Hump's, sent from the Sixth Regiment. Bussey spelled out that his camp was close to a tapioca plantation. His arrangement with the owner set him and his boys up with food and necessities. He asked us to come to him and he could make the arrangements for our departure in a submarine from the east coast of Malaya and he would go with us.

Hump, Saltz and I were excited and a meeting with Lao Woo followed. After the letter was translated to him, he asked what we wanted to do. We told him we would like to go to Bussey, instead of the Second Detachment. He stated he couldn't go with us, but we could go if that was our desire.

That is the way it stands now. We leave with Lao Woo tomorrow night, head north following the railroad and then continue on with a guerrilla force toward Bussey, while he goes on to the Second Detachment. Bussey sent a carton of Semangats cigarettes and a bottle of brandy. We washed, ate pineapple and a good meal, then took off up into the jungle to sleep, with our brandy as a bug chaser. Slept on the ground and bugs bit the hell out of me—little sleep.

June 29, 1945—Never did mention about eating frogs while staying at the Sixth Regiment. The Sakai and bodyguards went up the river at night and killed them by using a torch and club. Some were over eighteen inches long and extremely large. Very delicious!

Our departure was hampered by heavy rain. It came down in sheets, while we sat tight waiting for a break. At 1830, we hit the trail. Our party started with twenty-five men. Within the hour we found ourselves at another guerrilla post and waited again—four and a half hours—for the rain to slow.

At midnight our party of eight headed north, traveling along the railroad. We arrived at a farmhouse near Kampong Krau at 0500. Here I had another bad attack of the stomach cramps and fever. I took the quinine and prayed I wouldn't come down with a serious case.

The Chinese provided wonderful hospitality, offering us cigarettes, fresh fruits, five chickens, eggs, cookies and other delicacies. Our Communist leader, Lao Woo, appeared to carry a lot of weight!

During the day, preparations were made for us to cross the Pahang River. Lao Woo would push north to the Second Detachment. We thanked him and bid one another farewell, parting at 1830.

Crossing the railroad and the road running north to Jerantut, we made it to the shore of the Pahang River. It was as big as the Mississippi back home and had a very strong current. We were sampaned across the river, walked an hour and bedded down at a Chinese farmhouse.

The next two days we walked through swamp, bog, leeches and dense vegetation. First day, a nine-hour journey became twelve hours when our escort, Wee Ming, lost his way. When I figure that we trekked six hundred miles on our journey, I wonder how many of the miles were unnecessary due to the Chinese Communists' inability to know which way to go and admit it.

The evening of July 2, after an exhausting day fighting insect bites and leeches while trudging waist

Pahang River

deep in swamp water, we broke through the thick jungle and entered a large plantation. Wee Ming ordered his two guards to wait at the swamp's edge until he returned.

Contact was made with a Chinese worker who escorted our party to his quarters, then set out to give word to his boss at the plantation office.

"I'm a little nervous," Saltz said. "What if he brings the Japs?"

"Hump, let's play it safe and get under cover," I said.

"Okay! Duff, you and Saltz post yourselves about fifty feet south, behind a tree. I'll head in the other direction with Wee Ming, and do the same. We'll sit tight and see what develops. If it's a trap we'll rendezvous at the farmhouse we passed this evening."

"Got it, Hump. Let's go, Saltz."

A few steps placed us in the black of night, unseen from the dimly lit sleeping quarters. From our lookout we could view anyone approaching the shack and slip away if necessary. We crouched beside a tree and waited.

"How's the stomach, Duff?" Saltz asked.

"Not too good! The cramps and pain are giving me hell."

"What do you think it is?"

"I worry it's the appendix."

"You won't make it if it ruptures, Duff!"

"Thanks for reminding me!"

"Sorry, didn't mean to upset you."

"I know."

"Duff, you've amazed Hump and me."

"How's that?"

"Your spirit and determination. Ever since you got ill February 1—wasn't it?"

"Yeah, five months yesterday."

"Since then you've faced typhoid, cholera, beriberi, malaria fevers and chills, the stomach cramps and pains, your digestive tract giving you fits, the blow to your chest that probably broke a few ribs, maybe popped a hole in a lung, and you've lost over sixty pounds!"

"What are you getting at, Saltz?"

"Hump and I can't believe you're still alive!"

"Hope I haven't disappointed the two of you!"

"No, we like you just the same."

"Thanks! I like you too." We shared a laugh.

"Duff, how have you done it? I mean, Carl died in eight days and you've trekked six hundred miles. When you showed up at Woo Ping's camp sixty pounds light, you honestly looked like you wouldn't live through the night. Granted you've gained a few pounds back, but many days I thought it would be your last. You should be dead. Seriously—how have you pulled it off?"

"I rely on a few methods, Saltz. Are you sure you want to hear?"

"Of course . . . I'm asking, aren't I?"

"I pray. I've called on God to pull me through. I pray for strength, courage and God's guiding hand, and then I work at taking each step, knowing I have a role in my survival. Also, I think of Peggy and my son and daughter, knowing they're counting on me to return. Does my talk of God upset you?"

"It isn't a subject I care too much for, but I'm okay with your answer. Go on, what else?"

"I'm not trying to convert you, Saltz, I'm talking about me—okay?"

"I understand! I asked, remember?"

"When Carl died, I knew I was dying too! Remember how much sicker I was—compared to Carl?"

"Yeah."

"I lay beside Carl's dead body, shooing bugs and insects away from it for five hours. During that time I felt sorry for myself. I cried for Carl and me—and I believed I was about to join him. I saw the mask of death on Carl's face. I remember thinking about Peggy and our two children and how they would have to get along without me. I thought of how Peggy would never know how I died, or my last thoughts of my love for her. I got mad, Saltz! I lay on that sapling bed with Carl's body and I decided I would not die on that bed! I would die on my feet walking back to Peggy—if I were to die. Then, I prayed. I prayed for God to give me a hand, to help me, because I couldn't do it alone. Saltz—since that prayer—I knew I was going to make it. Sure, I have moments and days when I think it's my last, but then I remember and call on God and He gives me strength!"

"Gee—you're spooking me with this God stuff. Are you saying you felt God—I mean—God was there?"

"God is here! Right here with you and me, with Hump, with the Chinese. He's with everyone and everywhere." Saltz swept the area with his eyes and I chuckled.

"I'm sorry, Saltz! I wasn't laughing at you. It's just the way you looked around to see if God was here. I see God in people and in their actions. Remember

Peggy Duffy

how the Sakai went out of their way to help us, with their gifts of goats and chickens and their protection?"

"Yeah, what's that got to do with it?"

"I see the Sakai as an answer to prayer. Feeding, protecting, sheltering the three of us. And as much as I despise the Communists and their phony propaganda, I see God working through them. Food, protection, shelter—see what I mean? The Sakai and the Chinese don't have to help us! I mean, what are they getting out of the deal? We have nothing to give them in return. Sure, we've told the Communists our government will give them guns and ammunition, but the fact remains: they have helped us and kept us alive. I'm saying God works this way. We see people helping us, saving our tail end, but why? Why help us? Could it be God's hand working through these people? This is where faith and trust come into play. We aren't powerful enough to do this on our own, we need these people and maybe they need us."

"Need us?"

"Sure. Haven't we brought them another way of life, besides Communism? By sharing our philosophy of a democratic society, haven't we carried a message that possibly will change the lives of some of these men and boys—and Malaya? What I'm saying is that we, too, are working for God by sharing our beliefs and ourselves. Just like I have been sharing God with you! God uses us to help others. We see people helping us, but it is God's hand working through them . . . God at work."

"Duff, this is too deep for me. I've lived a life pretty much on my own without God, and I've done just fine. It's difficult to accept that God is here and there, or in people."

"Even in you!"

"Let's stop here! I've heard enough. 'God in him, God over there, God in me!' It gives me the creeps. How can you know when God is here? Or how can you get away from God, when you can't even see God? I mean here's some invisible guy lurking around and you can't see him. It makes me nervous. I'd always be looking over my shoulder wondering where the guy is. I don't like it."

I smiled and said, "Saltz, God is not someone you have lurking over your shoulder. He's not an invisible guy following or checking up on you. Try this: Whenever you see something that captures your attention, something majestic or beautiful, think of God."

"Like a beautiful woman?"

"Well, that's not what I had in mind, but a woman would work."

"So, when I see a beautiful woman think of God?"

"Right. God's awesome beauty and presence in our lives."

"Great, Duff, now you did it."

"Did what?"

"You just distorted my vision of women. Now, when I see a beautiful woman who puts a skip in my step, I might picture this God character looking back at me, whether I believe your God stuff or not."

"Saltz, it's not like that!"

I started laughing and couldn't stop. Every time I tried to say something I laughed harder. Not even the cramps or chest pain made me stop.

Saltz, though, had his pouting look, like he had just lost his dog or best friend. He quit talking to me and I kept laughing each time we made eye contact.

We sat for two hours before a party of three arrived at the workers quarters, our messenger and two others. They looked for us inside the quarters, then glanced back and forth searching the grounds.

Hump and Wee Ming approached them, Hump pointing his .45 and Wee Ming an old shotgun. Saltz and I gripped our .45s and crept up behind them before they were even aware of our presence.

"Good evening, I am Ng Teong Yiok. We have expected you for many months."

Yiok was about thirty years old, of slender build, about five feet five inches. He wore a smile on a tired, weathered face, and was dressed in a light-colored shirt, trousers and sandals. The third man was his aide.

"We are happy to meet you!" Hump said. "This is Wee Ming with the Malayan People's Anti-Jap Army. This is Lieutenant Duffy, Lieutenant Saltzman and I am Major Humphrey." We exchanged bows.

"You gentlemen must come to my home and we will have food and brandy."

"Wee Ming, what about your two men waiting at the swamp?" Hump asked.

"They will wait until I return."

He could have at least called them in from the disgusting swamp and put food in their stomachs. Once again, the disdain of Communist leaders for the rank and file. I was glad we were parting with the Communist leaders and their double standards.

It was a mile to the main house. We passed the

plantation office situated along the west side of the Kuantan-Kuala Lipis Road. A narrow, T-shaped building with a U-shaped drive at its front entrance, it reminded me of a roadhouse motel.

The motor road was pitch black. We crossed, and two hundred yards farther arrived at Yiok's wood frame house and slipped inside.

"Bring chicken, rice, tapioca and tea!" Yiok called to a servant. He poured a quarter glass of brandy for each man and raised his glass high.

"My American friends, a toast to the war's end!"

"To the war's end!" we repeated and downed the brandy. It set my throat and stomach on fire and its burning lingered. Yiok grabbed three bottles of brandy and led us into the dining room.

"Please sit!" he said.

We sat on cushioned chairs—in our swamp-covered clothes—around a marvelous hand-carved teak dining table. It was six months since I had enjoyed the comfort of a chair. The walls held paintings and items of Chinese cultural and local interest. An oriental rug covered the wood floor beneath the table, and there were glass windows. Electric lights were rigged to a generator. In an adjoining sitting room, there was a sofa and more upholstered chairs. I imagined leaving the table, walking into the next room and lying on the lush sofa, where I would stay until morning. I could almost feel its softness.

"Mr. Yiok, is Bussey here?" Hump asked.

"No, he is at camp deep in the jungle. I forwarded a message of your arrival before meeting you this evening. I expect him here tomorrow."

"This is quite an operation you have. How many acres is your plantation?" I asked.

"This plantation has four thousand acres of tapioca."

"You have other plantations?"

"My brother, Ng Teong Kiat, owns many businesses. There are the rubber, tapioca and jelutong plantations, jelutong factory, rubber works, sawmills, oil mills, biscuit factory, trading company and the Cameron Highlands plantations." Hump, Saltz and I stared at Yiok, wondering if he was serious.

"Your brother owns all these businesses?" Hump asked.

"Oh, yes, and I am his business partner."

"Haven't the Japs taken control of operations or shut you down?" I asked.

"No, the Japanese believe we are trusted friends. We supply them with our products and they pay my brother and me good money. Then, we take the money and support any groups or individuals fighting or sabotaging the Japs—Allied refugees, guerrilla forces, civilians, any operators known to be saboteurs to the Jap. We are fighting the Japs with their own money. This way our country still has goods and materials to help reduce shortages and hardship on our people, while we secretly pour money into resistance of the Japanese."

"I'll be damned!" Hump mumbled.

"Don't the Japs suspect anything?" I asked.

"No, we have become good collaborators and they trust us. This allows us to employ over one hundred friends and neighbors at this plantation. We provide food and shelter, they provide us with what we must accomplish here. They are grateful and so are we. My brother and I would make no money without our enterprise and it serves no good to hoard this Japanese banana money. What could be greater than helping our people and financing any person willing to resist these savage animals?"

I liked this guy and his operation!

"Banana money—what do you mean?" Saltz asked.

Yiok laughed, and pulled a roll of bills from his trouser pocket. He passed a bill to each of us and said, "See the stalk of bananas on the face of this Jap money?"

"Yes," we answered.

"Banana money! We call it banana because of the ridiculous attempt the Japs make to pass this off as Malayan currency, by picturing a commodity of our country. It is a poor attempt at manipulation of our people to accept the Jap, and their money as our money. Whether it was or wasn't their intention, this is how many Malayans feel when they refer to it. Do you understand?"

"Yes, I do," Saltz said.

We tried to pass the money back to Yiok but he said, "No, you keep it."

"Do you help finance the Communist guerrillas?" I asked. Yiok looked at Wee Ming as he answered me.

"Only the guerrillas who fight the Japs. Not those that sit back and talk about the Communist utopia that will come to be, once the Japs and English are cast out of our land."

Wee Ming was visibly upset by his comment, but did not challenge Yiok. Later we learned that the

"Banana money"

Japanese currency in occupied Malaya, 1942–1945.

millionaire brothers did not support the Communist Sixth Regiment for this reason.

"Yiok, where is your brother?" I asked.

"Kiat is in Kuala Lumpur tending to business. He is not one for the rigors of plantation and jungle life. Kiat prefers the comfort of the city."

"Kuala Lumpur—isn't that Jap headquarters for mainland Malaya?"

"Yes, but he is well received by the Japs. My brother serves their needs and provides supplies. He is valuable to them. He funnels Jap money back to the plantation and it finds its way to the resistance forces, which Kiat wants little to do with. He prefers to be in the dark about our activity. He is a great worrier and it irritates his stomach."

This reminded me of my stomach, and I asked Yiok, "Is there a doctor I can see? I have a problem with my stomach."

"Jerantut is the closest town with a doctor, but I don't know who we can trust. I would fear for our safety."

Before the meal, I asked to be excused. Painful cramps and fever left no appetite. Yiok set me up with quinine and had his aide guide me to a supply hut, where blankets and cushions were spread on the floor for Hump, Saltz, Wee Ming and me. That was 0100. I was out before hitting the floor after this brutal day.

Two hours had passed when Hump stumbled and fell on top of me. He and Saltz were weaving from brandy mixed with exhaustion. Their laughing and loud talk lasted five minutes, then they crashed and burned.

J. Jack Bussey

J. Jack Bussey

In the morning, seated on the cushioned chairs around Yiok's dining table, we enjoyed a breakfast of eggs, fish, rice, pineapple, banana, tapioca and coffee. I could have sat in that chair for days!

We were sipping coffee and sharing our story with Yiok, when his aide entered and whispered to him. He looked up and announced, "The Captain has arrived."

We had just stood when the kitchen door swung open and in walked J. Jack Bussey and three Chinese lads, about nineteen or twenty years old.

"Damn it fellows, I'm glad to see you!" Bussey said. "What the hell took you so long to get here? Don't you know I've been waiting since January and I haven't seen nor spoken to an American since December? This is cause for celebration! We need some brandy. Get each of us a bottle of brandy!"

This guy was a character. He wore an Australian hat and shirt, American Army pants and boots, and a thick black beard. A Thompson machine gun was in his right hand, a carbine over his shoulder, .45-caliber handgun holstered around his waist, along with a machete, two hand grenades clipped to his belt, and a cigarette hanging from his lips.

We stared and listened to his rambling voice while we took in all the details of his appearance. He looked like a war machine!

His three Chinese boys were dressed in American pants, shirts and boots. All held carbines and had grenades clipped to their belts. Their names were "Khaki," "Angry" and "Yapper."

Khaki was a tough looking lad and tallest of the three. Angry was effeminate looking and soft spoken. Yapper was big, brave and stupid. All were devoted and trusted comrades of Bussey.

"Bussey, this is Wee Ming, our guide from the Sixth Regiment," Hump said. "We would like to take care of business, so he can be on his way. Wee Ming tells us you made an agreement with the guerrillas to pay them guns and money for delivering us to you."

"Wee Ming, glad to meet you! I owe you some money for bringing our boys."

Bussey reached in his breast pocket and pulled out a wad of money. Then he signaled Khaki, who came forward, opened a cloth pouch and spilled gold coins on the table.

"Here is thirty thousand Jap dollars, three thousand Thai dollars, and fifteen gold pieces. This should cover our agreement."

Yapper, Khaki, & Angry

"What about the guns?" Wee Ming asked.

"We are waiting for Allied Headquarters in Ceylon to make the parachute drop which will deliver your carbines. You will have to be patient until then!"

"When will they come?"

"I would hope within five to seven days. We'll send word when they arrive."

"Your promise is for twenty-five rifles for each man delivered!"

"Yes, seventy-five guns, Wee Ming. But you have to wait just like we do."

Wee Ming, realizing there was nothing further he could do, turned to Hump and said, "Major, our agreement is fulfilled. You must now give me your pistols!" The three of us removed our shoulder holsters—with our .45 revolvers—and passed them to Wee Ming.

"Major Humphrey, Lieutenant Duffy, Lieutenant Saltzman, thank you for keeping your word. I am grateful."

"Thank you for your help, Wee Ming. We wish you the best," Hump said.

He made it clear to Bussey that the guerrillas would return if there were no word, then departed. Once he passed through the door, Bussey spoke up.

"Why the hell did you give him your guns?"

"We made a deal back in January to turn them over once we reached our destination," Hump said.

"Your guns?"

"Yes, our guns. You promised the Communists twenty-five carbines for each of us?"

"Yes, we agreed on the price a couple days ago."

"Can you fill the order? Do you really have a parachute drop coming from SEAC?"

"No, but we'll take care of them. Let me handle it."

I wasn't sure what this meant, and I wondered how he intended to deliver. Time would tell.

"What was the deal with all the money?" I asked. "Where did that come from?"

"Yiok put up the Jap dollars and I had the rest. We offered them fifty thousand dollars to bring you boys."

"Yiok, thank you for your help," I said.

"Yes, thank you." Hump said. Saltz smiled and nodded his head. I couldn't believe the kindness and generosity of this man.

"Working with the guerrillas has been a joke," Bussey said. "One day they sent word you were coming. The next day you weren't coming. Then it would start over . . . you are coming, you aren't coming! Hell—the last I heard I think you weren't coming."

"We weren't too sure of their plans for us, either," Hump said. "We've been kept in the dark about most things involving them and their organization."

"Bussey, who are you tied up with? Army?" I asked.

"Actually, I'm assigned to the OSS—Office of Strategic Services. Intelligence."

"What's the OSS doing in Malaya?" Hump asked.

"Back on December 7, I parachuted with these three boys from a Liberator flown by the British, to locate a guy named Pat Noone. He is supposed to have taken off with the Sakai when the Japs invaded Malaya. He was riding in a car with a mining engineer named Len Coffey, who is now a lieutenant colonel in British

Intelligence, when the Japs ambushed them. Noone took off into the jungle and was not heard from again. Coffey managed to get to the city of Grik and get out of the country.

"The damn pilot of the Liberator dropped me eighty-six miles south of where I should have landed. Three of our six equipment parachutes didn't open and we lost a radio, guns, food and ammunition. But fortunately, we landed on the outskirts of Yiok's plantation."

"You have a radio, though, right?" I asked.

"Well, yeah, we have a radio, but it can't transmit right now, only receive."

"What? How the hell were you planning on contacting a sub to get us out of here?" Hump asked.

"I'm working on the radio and hope get it up and running. Any of you guys handy with a radio?"

"Bussey, you wrote us a letter stating you could get a sub to pick us up off the east coast of Malaya, and you would go with us!" Hump yelled. "Just how did you plan on accomplishing that?"

"The radio comes and goes. There's so much damn moisture and humidity, I can't seem to keep it clicking one day to the next."

"Oh, crap! We're hiking swamps and wrestling leeches to find out there isn't a radio? Isn't this dandy," Saltz said in disgust.

"Hey, guys—there's a radio and it does work, just not now."

"Have you ever transmitted?" I asked.

"Hell, yes! I tell you we can get this thing going. I just need some time and a good pair of hands."

"Hump, I'll take a look at it and see what I can do. I know enough about the mechanics of a radio that maybe I'll have some luck," Saltz said.

"You a radioman?" Bussey asked.

"Flight engineer, but I worked with our radioman, Mick, enough to know my way around."

"Where's this Mick guy?"

"Dead!" Saltz snapped.

"Sorry. How many of your boys are missing?"

"Eight," Hump said. "Four are dead and four were captured by the Japs and thrown in prison. We heard they were being starved. Our copilot and radioman died in the crash. Rear gunner Spratt was burned badly and died within the first couple days. Carl Hansman—our navigator—died from malaria, cholera and typhoid in a guerrilla camp one month after we landed."

"Awful sorry about your buddies."

"Bussey, where's your radio?" Hump asked.

"At camp, four hours from here. We'll go there soon enough, but right now let's enjoy this brandy and have a little celebration. It's the Fourth of July tomorrow."

"Have you made contact with the Second Detachment?" I asked.

"Second Detachment—what Second Detachment?" Bussey asked.

"The British and Aussies," I said.

"There's a detachment of British and Australians?"

"You don't know about them?" Hump asked.

"Hell no! You guys giving me a line of crap?"

"No, but you deserve it," Saltz said.

"Where's this detachment?"

"It's up the road from you, about fifty miles, between Jerantut and Kuala Lipis," Hump said. "That's where we were headed until you sent the love letter about a submarine."

"Come on, don't start on the damn radio again."

"You deserve it, you bastard!" Saltz yelled.

"Okay, let's all take a break and forget the radio for now," Hump said.

"So—the Second Detachment—when did they land?"

"February."

"February! I got boys operating fifty miles up the road and I'm just hearing about it? How did you find out?"

"They've been in touch with the Communist guerrillas. We heard while we were hooked up with the Sixth Regiment. They wanted us to go there instead of coming to you. Seems the guerrillas don't like you because you refuse to work with them," Hump said.

"You know, I don't like them either. I don't care for their Communist ideology and I don't want to be indebted to them."

"But now you owe them seventy-five carbines!"

The brandy was getting the best of them and a quarrel brewed. I had quit the brandy during the second glass, to nurse my stomach, and I tried to change the subject.

"Bussey, where are you from in the States?"

"My home is Maryville, Missouri."

"Your letter said you're operating under an alias. What's your real name?

"Franklin Bithos."

"What's a Bithos?" Saltz taunted.

"Saltz, cut the crap. Take a break," I said.

We continued to shoot the bull, eat all sorts of delicacies and consume brandy . . . except me. The party continued into the evening, when we were joined by some of Yiok's friends.

"Gentlemen, I introduce Chu Soo, the manager of our plantation, and Wong Su, who is the Number 1 contact man for the Japanese in Pahang."

"Contact man for the Japs?" Hump asked. We sat up and focused on this wide, fleshy man. Bussey ran up and threw his arms around him and gave a bear hug.

"Boys, this is one friend we can't do without," Bussey said. "Wong Su is Taiwanese, and his duties for the Japs are to inform them of any guerrilla or Allied agents in Pahang. He also knows days in advance of any Jap troops moving into the area and he's friends with a Jap colonel, who stops by his home each morning for coffee and sweets."

The man cocked a smile as Bussey—by now in the bag—wrapped an arm around his shoulders and continued. "Wong Su drives a vehicle with Jap military plates. He drives where he pleases and is not subject to police search."

We stood and greeted Yiok's guests and exchanged bows of respect.

Between Yiok and Wong Su, they had knowledge of any moves the Japs made in their area. If a search was scheduled, Wong Su would pass the word and the Japs never seemed to arrive at a time when a guerrilla, spy or saboteur was present.

July 4, 1945—A wonderful feast took place and Bussey brought out opium afterward. All of us smoked some for the experience and I can see how it would make you an addict. Bussey parachuted in with $100,000 worth of opium and $400,000 in Jap money. The opium and money were to help him buy troops, information and supplies. Tools to carry out his work provided by the Office of Strategic Services.

Quite a party and again I had to retire early. Damn stomach and fever. We slept across the road at Chu's farmhouse. Hump had quite a time of it. Mighty drunk out tonight.

July 5, 1945—Left at noon for J. Jack's camp and arrived around 1600. Many foodstuffs with our party and a lot of climbing. Made the trip okay with no stomach trouble.

Quite a nice camp. There is a clear water stream right in front of camp. Good for cooking and bathing. I guess I'll take cold showers for the rest of my life. We have one large hut with a bed running the length of it. All the men who are employed here, about eighteen, live there. We sleep in a section of another hut, which has four partitions or rooms. We're on the end. Khaki, Angry, and Yapper share the next. Then a store room, and last is where the two women and this one-year-old baby girl sleep. Why Bussey let these two women and baby girl live here is beyond me.

We're sleeping on one of the best bamboo beds we've had and there's no mosquitoes. We have a roost for the chickens and ducks, which are plentiful and it makes me want to have a farm someday. A nice little shack for cooking, where they have one of those large Chinese pans that is used for all purposes.

Across the water and upstream there is another large grass shack, which hasn't been completed as yet. Farther up is another camp that J. Jack built in case of a Jap visit.

Bussey's camp is entirely different than the Communists'. Here these lazy bastards play some chipped card game all day long, and Chinese music from a phonograph drives you crazy.

Food adequate. Feeling bad tonight. Have a fever of 102. Ten sulfadiazine tablets and atabrine made up the following day and 103.5 fever. Still, I feared the appendix. Praying if it is, it not rupture. The infection from a rupture would eat the wall of the abdominal cavity, intestine, spleen, pancreas, and stomach. One would be fortunate to die quick.

"Bussey, I want to take a look at that radio," Saltz said.

Bussey had Khaki bring the radio from the supply room. Hump and I stood over Saltz and Bussey while they discussed electronic jargon, and poked and pointed at the radio.

"Have at it, Saltzman. Do what you can, you've got my blessing."

"Damn glad I got your blessing, Bussey!"

These two took every opportunity to disagree and take jabs, especially Saltz.

Bussey outranked Saltz and me—captain to first lieutenants—and liked being in charge. Results usually were sarcasm and defiance on Saltz's part.

We hadn't used rank too much the past six months and we were Army Air Corps, Bussey was OSS. We fell under Humphrey's command, not Bussey's. Hump let it ride for the most part.

Hump and I let Saltz tinker with the radio while we washed up in the stream. When we returned Saltz was ready to explode.

"How's it going, Saltz?" Hump asked. "Any chance at getting the transmitter back?"

"No—the transmitter literally 'bit the dirt' when Bussey landed. I don't think he's been able to transmit since he hit the jungle. He has one frequency that's good, 6210. The receiver is in fine shape to give us news, but this radio will not get us out of Malaya."

We had had our share of disappointments over the past six months. Every attempt at rescue failed miserably. I guess we couldn't blame Bussey for our latest defeat. He wanted our company. Sure, we were on his back for a while because of his radio and submarine story, but we were alive and his setup with Yiok and the plantation was a good one.

"We need to make contact with the Second Detachment. It doesn't appear Malaya will be on the Allies' agenda too soon," Hump said.

"It looks like the war could last another three months," I said. "Who's going to make the trip?"

"I need to go!" Bussey said. "I've got to make contact and set coordinates and dates for parachute drops with South East Asia Command. Once they confirm I'm still alive we'll have a radio, rations, medical supplies and arms dropped right in our laps."

"I'll go too," Hump said. "I'll see that our names and serial numbers reach the Twentieth Bomber Command. Duff, I'll advise them how serious your stomach and chest injuries are and see if they can evacuate us on the double."

"Sounds good, Hump."

I knew if my appendix was the problem and it ruptured, I was a goner. And I saw little hope of a submarine and our party rendezvousing any time soon.

I prayed.

Bussey's Camp

July 9, 1945—Bussey, Hump, Yapper and two bearers departed at noon for the Second Detachment. We believe Bussey's radio is no good and our only hope of getting out of Malaya is for the Second Detachment to make the necessary arrangements. It will probably take one month, possibly more. In their absence, Saltz and I are in command of Bussey's camp with the assistance of Khaki and Angry.

Just before Bussey left, he pulled Saltz and me aside and pointed out one of his Chinese boys, who he believes is a Jap detective. He's trying to gather evidence before making a move on him. He's not to leave camp under any circumstances.

They took three carbines, three .45s, and three hand grenades. Personally, I don't get it. We have about fifteen men and two women here besides Saltz, Khaki, Angry, and myself. Our armament is four carbines, one tommy gun, one .45-caliber, three hand grenades, and two .45s in town. We'll be in sad shape if the Japs start searching the area.

July 11, 1945—Six months in Malaya today and still the redhead doesn't know I'm alive—God pity her and the little ones. I know by her faith and fidelity, she will feel I'm still with her. I'll be back, Red darling, no matter how many illnesses I encounter.

A little playing around went on last few nights between Khaki and these two women. Angry told me a few of his experiences and the sex discussion that took place after hitting the sack is one that I'll never forget. These Chinese boys sure like their debauchery and they think nothing of having an affair with another man's wife or contracting some social disease. Amazing individuals!

Dreamed of Peg and my folks last night and I didn't want to get up, it was so real—maybe it's a good sign—I hope and pray. My sister Lorraine's birthday today.

July 16, 1945—We keep sending men in to the plantation for vegetables and keep hearing from Hump and Bussey. They haven't departed. They are waiting for the Communists to send letters all over Malaya, to receive the coordinates of Second Detachment and safe passage.

We tuned the radio to 6210 and learned the B-29's came to Kuala Lumpur and dropped leaflets telling the people to spend all their Jap money for food, etc. In the Philippines the Jap money is no longer any good and it wouldn't be any good in Malaya. They said the Allies were coming very soon!

Dream of Peg and my folks nearly every night. I'll say

one thing, Peg is in for some heavy loving when I get back!

"Saltz, listen to Hump's letter about the wild pig."

"Go ahead."

'Hope you got the wild pig we sent. Yapper was hunting, standing on a big log at the edge of the jungle where the plantation's wood potatoes begin. Yap heard wild pigs in the potatoes and saw ten or twelve coming toward him, heading for the jungle. He was waiting for the first one to get closer when a huge tiger leaped from behind him, nailed the lead pig by the throat, and jumped back into the jungle with the squealing pig in its jaws. Yap saw the tiger twenty yards in and fired two rounds. The tiger jumped six to eight feet and took off. He stood two feet high and was mighty big. Paw tracks were the size of my hand. I arrived and waited a few minutes before I walked in and found the dead pig. One ear was missing and there were about twelve holes where the tiger had sunk its teeth in the pig's throat. The holes were two inches deep, but there was very little blood. We dragged it to the clearing and two plantation boys carried it to Kiat's on poles. It must have weighed 150 pounds. Well, enjoy the meal, boys!'

"I'll bet the tiger is still mad about losing the pig," Saltz said.

"Can you imagine it bounding away carrying a 150-pound pig in its jaw?" I asked. "Yapper is damn lucky the tiger didn't take him in place of the pig!"

July 20, 1945—Note from our two boys in the plantation told they left for Second Detachment evening of the 18th.

Worst attack I've had in my stomach last night and

all today. Can't stretch my arms or legs without sharp pains. It seems to have localized in appendix area and where I injured myself on bailing out. Realize it rests in Our Lord's hands from here on out—Sulfadiazine has no more effect on the pain. I hope they have a medical man with the Second Detachment. Trying my utmost to forget what the consequences will be in case anything should happen. I know Peg is a capable woman, will manage beautifully, and will be a good mother to our two children.

The Agent—who is in solid with Chu, the plantation manager, and has the two women and baby staying in our camp—rolled in at 0730 this morning. Bussey has him on his payroll—$700 month—as an outside informer who picks up news around the village, which is made up of coolie workers for the plantation and their families.

He informed Saltz and me the "Big Son," Wong Song King, was at the manager's house and wanted to see us tonight. He's Yiok's nephew and the son of Kiat.

Leaving Angry to care for things and monitor the radio receiver, Saltz and I took off with the Agent, Khaki, and Drinkwater.

Drinkwater got his name on account of the Japs making him drink gallon upon gallon of water when caught as a bearer for the guerrillas. He was also shot twice. Remarkable!

We met Shorty halfway to the plantation and turned Drinkwater around, returning him to camp with the vegetables Shorty carried. Drinkwater was a good worker, but has a problem with opium. It was best he not be left unattended at the plantation or village. He could be an easy target to sell information.

Shorty, always smiling, is our most dependable bearer and a damn good boy. He and Slim, assigned to Bussey by Yiok, are devoted to their task and fully cooperate with us. They are true patriots of Malaya.

Slim is being paid $400 month, Shorty $200 month and "Serious" or Lim Bunn—Bussey's pride and joy—$400 month. Most of the other boys in camp receive $150 month.

Slim is the best man for your money. He was on his way to camp with a message one morning when a poisonous snake bit him shortly after he left the plantation. Instead of turning back, he made the four-hour trip in six, crawling on hand and knees at the end. He arrived suffering terribly and soon became delirious and lapsed into a coma. The following day, when he was out of danger and able to talk, he was asked why he didn't return to the plantation, since he received the poisonous bite early in the journey. His reply: "I didn't care whether I lived or died, just so I was able to fulfill my duty."

Saltz and I arrived at the plantation and were waiting for twilight before crossing the road to Chu's farmhouse when Yapper showed up from the Second Detachment.

"I have orders from the Captain."

"Go ahead, Yap," I said.

"Angry is to arm himself with a .45 revolver and head immediately to the Second Detachment carrying fifty thousand dollars in one hundred dollar bills and two fully charged, six-volt, forty-amp batteries. Captain says you should arrange for a car to transport him."

"What's going on, Yapper?" I asked.

"It's a poor setup. Things were bad when we arrived. The Second Detachment is staying in a camp of the Communists' Sixth Regiment, and a Captain Lao Woo is causing trouble. He threw a British machine gun to the ground, spit on it and told his guerrillas, 'We do not want British weapons! We are citizens of Malaya and these British and American officers are no good. They are enemies just as much as the Japanese. The Communist flag should be paramount in Malaya and I don't care what the British or Americans think!'

"He told me I didn't have a country and I am just a tool for the British and Americans. I took out my .45 and told him I would shoot the ass off him if he didn't watch his tongue."

Saltz and I smiled.

"Good job, Yap!" I said, patting his shoulder. "How about the fifty thousand dollars—what's that for?"

"Supplies for the guerrillas and British. Captain is trying to buy favor with Lao Woo." "What's the story on the batteries?" Saltz asked.

"Second Detachment is having trouble with their generator."

"How about the radio, did they transmit to South East Asia Command?" Saltz asked.

"Yes, names and serial numbers were radioed and they have requested a submarine. Major Humphrey says he will wait for the departure date and location.

"There is an Indian doctor with them. Major explained symptoms of your illness and the doctor believes all your trouble is due to your injury affecting your diaphragm. He said this will cause you pain all through your waist, but he can not be sure without X-rays!"

"I hope he's right," I said. That would ease my fears. "Rest up, Yapper. First sign of morning light head to camp, relay your orders to Angry and return with him. Leave Slim in charge and have Sweet Potato lend a hand with the batteries." Sweet Potato was a bruiser. He was another good and dependable bearer.

Twilight came and we crossed the road to the manager's house. Inside, Chu, Yiok, Wong Su and Big Son sat at a table waiting for us to join them for dinner.

With Saltz and me seated, Mrs. Chu served duck and rice while Yiok introduced his nephew. He was round and wide, dressed in a white pants and a brown button-down shirt.

"Gentlemen, my uncle has told me of your misfortune and hardship. I hope since you have come to our plantation your stay has been good."

"Yes, it has," Saltz said. "Your uncle is a good man." Yiok smiled and nodded his head in appreciation.

"Why did you send for us?" I asked.

"I need your help. The Japs have had my father under surveillance for the past few weeks. He and other business leaders believe the invasion of Malaya is on its way, and feel the Japs will execute them beforehand. He wishes to hide at the Captain's camp for safekeeping. Will you help him?"

"Of course! We'll take good care of him," I said. Heck, this was the man whose food, money and shelter were keeping us alive.

"There is something else. You have a Chinese detective working with the Japs at your camp."

"Bussey said he may be working for the Japs, but he isn't sure," I said.

"This man cannot be there when my father arrives. It's too dangerous."

"What do you want to do with him?" Saltz asked.

"Kill him!" Big Son said.

"We don't know if he's guilty," I said.

"Many believe he is guilty. Even his uncle, Wong Su."

"Wong Su, this man is your nephew?" I asked.

"Yes. I have heard he was sent by the Japs."

I couldn't believe my ears. The guy's own uncle was out to get him. The callous nature of Wong Su and Big Son was disturbing.

"What do you say we wait until we have evidence? We can get a note off to Bussey and hear back in plenty of time before your father arrives," I said. "A few days won't hurt. The man has lived in the camp for two months—what's a couple days?"

"I agree," Saltz said. "Let's take it slow. He's got a few buddies in camp, and Bussey's their commander. They may see us as exercising undue authority if we try to stage an execution. Besides, he isn't going anywhere."

"Okay, we will wait," Big Son said. "But if my father arrives, we execute him."

Saltz and I didn't know what to say.

The following morning, Angry and Yapper—dressed in civilian clothes—took Big Son's car and transported Bussey's batteries, $50,000 and our message. Can you imagine getting away with this in a Jap-occupied country?

July 30, 1945—News reported MacArthur and Mountbatten met in Manila and Malaya is on the program. Big three—Truman, Stalin and Churchill—met in Potsdam, six miles from Berlin, to discuss the future of Germany. Japan on its last legs and our fleet, B-29s, and fighters are playing hell with the little yellow bastards.

The Labor Party won in England and Winston Churchill is no longer Prime Minister. Russia's Joe 'the bastard' Stalin also refused to fight Japan, but he'll want some of the gravy.

America's Congress is supposed to have adopted the policies of the World Peace Conference and is going to support the International Security Army.

Bussey's promise of twenty-five carbines for each of us has started to rebound, because he hasn't produced them and the guerrillas are furious. They have five men stationed in the village with instructions to keep a check on us and see if we have supplies dropped by airplane. They won't do anything to us until they find out they aren't going to receive the guns and so far it looks like we won't be able to produce them. We'll have to sit tight and see what develops.

We really have some worthless men in this outfit, and I think Bussey had his head up his bucket when he let all these characters come into this camp. With the exception of the men I mentioned, most of these guys are lazy and cannot be trusted.

Have eaten dog—which isn't too hot—and octopus since I've been here. Bean shoots, eggs, wild boar, beef, fowl, mein fon and rice is our steady diet. Pineapples, papaya and bananas roll in frequently. Coffee and tea any hour of the day. A wonderful setup!

August 1, 1945—Note from Saltz, along with a note he received from Bussey, arrived in camp from the plantation. Bussey gave us "orders"(mind you) to shoot the detective. Well, Saltz told me he thought Bussey was drunk when he wrote the letter. Personally, I agree with Saltz, so we will hold off the execution. We in turn sent a note off to Hump to get his input on the Jap detective before proceeding.

Bussey wrote that we should forward the gas generator and essentials for running it. No longer do we get the news in the evening, as that powers our receiver. He also stated that he has received the "Silver Star," quite an honor—more power to him.

"Arrangements must be made for Kiat's arrival," Khaki told Saltz and me.

"What arrangements?" Saltz asked.

"The richest man in Malaya is also the fattest man in Malaya," Khaki said. "He brings an Indian cook to prepare his meals and he wishes to dine alone."

"Does he inhale food, like his son?" Saltz asked.

"Yes, he has a large appetite! Between Big Son and Kiat there could be a foodstuff shortage."

"What else?" I asked.

"Kiat will insist on private quarters. He wants to be alone, isolated as much as possible. He will demand a latrine and bathing area where no one will see him."

"Because of his weight?" I asked.

"No, there is another reason."

"Let's hear it," I said.

"This is a story of how the richest man in Malaya came into power. Ng Teong Kiat was a young man when he came to Malaya from China. Soon after arriving he met a woman who was a very wealthy prostitute. Kiat asked her to marry him, but first she made him swear he had no other wives. Kiat swore there were no others and the two wed. Time passed and Kiat began all these businesses and was making quite a name and fortune for himself.

"It turns out Kiat had married before coming to Malaya, and finally sent for his wife living in China. Well, the prostitute got wind of this and began to rant and rave. She became very upset with Kiat, out of her mind, hysterical. The relationship deteriorated, and Kiat refused to sleep with her. One night Kiat did go to her home and spent the night in her bed. While Kiat was sleeping this woman took a sharp knife and cut his penis or sack off."

I cringed. "Khaki, you're not serious!"

"Oh yes, this is true, every bit."

"That's terrible!" I said. "That's the worst story I've ever heard. What happened to the guy, I mean what kind of damage did she do?"

"Major damage!" Saltz snickered. "He was neutered. We're talking pain. Cries could be heard in China!"

The three of us had been sitting on the ground in the clearing and now lay on our backs laughing.

"Can you imagine that?" I asked. "You're sleeping and suddenly awaken to this excruciating pain in your groin—what happen to Kiat after she cut him off?"

"Literally!" Saltz said.

"Kiat ran to a doctor and the doctor did some repairs. I don't know how good a job was done, but he had to adopt all three of his sons, and he doesn't want to be seen naked. Afterward, the woman was so upset that she drowned herself in a well," Khaki added.

"It sounds like a story the author of *Exotic Edna* would write," Saltz said.

August 6, 1945—These Chinese in Bussey's camp are the most peculiar and astonishing people in the world. They love their sex and have no scruples about having another man's wife. All their songs concern sex and the talk that goes on between man and woman would embarrass the lowest character in the States. They grab each other's privates with other people looking on and it means nothing to either sex to be told they have too much intercourse—of course they don't use the word intercourse! Three wives is common and the more money, the more wives. It is disgusting as well as enlightening.

Saltz and I talked till four in the morning and we touched on every subject in the books. Religion was the main discussion and both profited by the discussion. I feel as though a closer bond is existent between us, more and more each day. I'm really grateful for this opportunity we've had—being left in Bussey's camp. We have had to make important decisions and we've seen eye to eye on most. A profitable experience.

Wong Su took Angry with the generator in his car so there wouldn't be any trouble with the Japs. If caught, Wong and Yiok's punishment for covert activity against the Japs is execution. Still, these two men looked beyond, to how they could serve their family, friends, neighbors and country in the daily hardship they faced.

Khaki and I trekked to the plantation on the morn of August 8, with the intention of escorting Kiat to our camp. We decided if we didn't hear from Hump before the old man came to camp, I would dispatch Slim from the village and the detective would be executed. This left all the dirty work on Saltz's hands, but he wanted it that way. War is ironic, at times.

Yiok had no word of when to expect Kiat from Kuala Lumpur.

We were at the manager's house when Slim and Shorty came over and stated Bussey was at mile 61—along the motor road—we were at mile 87. We tried to arrange a car for him, but the battery was dead. Instead we dispatched Sweet Potato, Slim, and one of the manager's men on bicycles to meet him.

I wonder what to expect. . . .

Bill & J Jack.

Received ~~your letter~~ last evening but due to the rain it was unreadable with the exception of that sentence informing me that it was HQ's order that the ~~detective~~ detective be executed. He was shot at 0640 and everything went well and contrary to my idea that we would have trouble burying him, we had plenty of assistance. Everything in the camp runs well and there is nothing to report. If there was any important things that yesterday's letter contained for me to do please repeat them as I unfortunately could get nothing from it in its condition. You mentioned something about J Jack coming here but missed that too.

Cliff.

What about the old man?

Saltzman's note to Duffy & J. Jack
reporting the execution of the Jap detective.

The Jap Detective

Bussey and the boys arrived at 0700 after a twenty-six mile bike ride through the night. Bussey, tired and dirty, wasted no time in confronting me on the detective.

"I heard the Jap detective is still alive. I ordered you to execute him eight days ago!"

"We got your message, but Saltz and I decided to wait. We were worried you were into the brandy when you sent the note."

"I gave an order!"

"We don't take orders from you, Bussey. If Hump had sent the note it would have been different. As it is, we met with Wong Su and Big Son, and agreed to hold off until we had evidence against the man or at least until Kiat arrived."

"Headquarters gave me orders to execute the Jap detective and take every precaution to insure old man Kiat's safety!"

"Headquarters gave the orders?"

"Yes, headquarters!"

"Fine—at least I know it's not the brandy making the decision. Saltz is standing by waiting my word. Slim can carry the message to camp and take Khaki's revolver to do the job."

"Slim, tell Saltzman to come to the plantation after the execution. You stay behind and take charge of the camp," Bussey ordered.

"Yes, Captain."

It was later I learned headquarters had not ordered Bussey to execute the detective. It had been his idea. His orders were to make sure old man Kiat was safe, so Bussey decided the Jap detective should die.

Damn Bussey! The whole stinking mess made me sick to my stomach. God, help us!

Bussey and I took shelter from a morning rain at Yiok's house, awaiting news of Kiat's arrival. Bussey had a portable receiver the Second Detachment had given him, replacing the one we lost when we issued them our generator.

"Turn on the receiver, it's been six days since we've had any news," I said. "Any word from South East Asia Command on our evacuation?"

"We have to sit tight until Malaya is liberated. Obviously, headquarters wouldn't radio any date or plan, but we understood their unspoken message. I think it's coming real soon, Duff! When it does, we'll be responsible for creating as much bedlam and destruction against the Japs as we can."

"What's the news on Hump, how come he didn't return with you?"

"He decided to stay with the Second Detachment and monitor the radio. In the meantime, you and Saltzman are to stay here. We have work to do."

"What kind of work?"

"We have to make a clearing for airplane drops, set up communications with the Second Detachment, and prepare for our role in the liberation of Malaya. And we'll need to appease the guerrillas and assure them their rifles will be delivered."

"Are the rifles being delivered?" I asked.

"I don't know."

Bussey's ideas tended to lack sufficient thought before put into action, and I feared he might jeopardize our safety down the road. I grew uneasy with each passing day. Still—this was his show.

Saltzman arrived about 1830 and Yiok had dinner served. Brandy was the main course and before Saltz got inebriated I asked him about the execution.

"Saltz, how did it go? Have any trouble with the detective's buddies?"

"No—no trouble with any of the boys! I was surprised."

"Not even 'The Muscle,' his brother, or 'The Movie Actor'?" These boys were big obstacles in Bussey's camp. All three were no good. The Muscle couldn't leave camp on account of his connections with the Communists of the Sixth Regiment. His brother, Low Fay, was defiant and irritating, pushing everyone's button. The Movie Actor spent his time dreaming or talking of his future in acting and was the best-groomed Chinaman living in the jungle. They didn't lift a finger the entire time Bussey was away. The three were a burden, and each was on the payroll at $150 month. I figured Bussey kept paying them because it wouldn't be safe to let them return to the village.

Saltz continued. "No, those boys tagged along and kept quiet. They probably realized that there were ways to address problems that crop up in camp. You know, like 'Maybe I'm next.'"

"Sure—just what they need, a picture of what their future could be."

"Yeah. Well, when Slim arrived I figured the order had been given and the detective's future looked bleak. Slim passed me the message and the .45. I read the note and was damn glad it was Bussey's decision, not yours or mine.

"I picked up a piece of cord and motioned for Slim and Shorty to follow me. We stepped out in the rain and crossed the clearing to the other *basha*. When I entered everyone grew silent and trained their eyes on the .45 I pointed. The detective looked up momentarily, then turned back to the playing cards he held in his hand.

"I crossed the floor and stopped in front of him and he looked up, but showed no expression. I could feel my heart pound and wondered if it was causing my shirt to rise and fall. My throat was dry and my hands clammy. It was the same kind of feeling you get going into a fistfight.

"Up to this point, I wasn't aware of the raindrops in my hair making their way down my cheek and dripping to the floor. I switched the gun to my other hand, to wipe my face and run my fingers through my hair, causing a lot of nervousness on the part of the bystanders. I guess they thought I was going to open up and plug a few of them where they stood. I felt more confident after their display of fear.

"Shorty stepped around me and asked the detective to point out his possessions. *'Wicker basket, two shirts, pair shorts, toothbrush, hair comb, tin cup and broken eyeglasses.'* Shorty placed them in the basket and shoved it under the sapling bed, then motioned him to stand. Slim took the cord and bound his hands behind his back.

"Meanwhile, I looked at the ten or twelve other men and boys seated or standing in the *basha*. Most eyes were fixed on the detective standing barefoot in shorts and a ragged tee shirt. Others watched me pointing the .45 at the thin man's side. The steady fall of rain was the only sound as we waited for Slim to finish tying the knots.

"With the detective bound, we pointed him toward the door. He followed Slim and Shorty, while I poked the .45 in his back. The remaining men followed at a close distance. A gallery formed to witness the detective's fate.

"Outside, we crossed the clearing and headed to the log over the stream. The rain continued but nobody seemed bothered. Two of our boys—"Sweet Potato" and "The Cripple"—jumped in line and took the lead, carrying hooked spades.

"Single file, we made our way across the stream and climbed the bank. Our gravediggers continued through the grass and brush another twenty yards, stopping in a small open area to begin digging.

"I watched Sweet Potato and the Cripple take turns making the grave. The Jap detective watched too. Imagine watching two men dig a grave, knowing that in a few minutes, this is where your body will lie covered with dirt.

"The soil was saturated and full of roots. Each scrape of the mud, water would seep in, leaving a black muddy pool at the bottom of the hole. I envisioned myself lying in the wet grave, covered with mud, and it sent a shiver through my body.

"Shorty pointed to a young tree a few feet from us and held a rope to tie the man. I nodded yes, and Shorty pushed the detective against the tree and wrapped the cord around his chest. Slim approached with a burlap bag and stood along side the Jap detective, while Shorty finished his knots.

"I said to Slim, 'Ask the man if he has anything to say before he dies.' His answer was, 'No. If I have to die, that's life.'

"I looked at the man's face. It held no expression, not even a blink of an eye.

"Just as Slim lifted the burlap bag over his head, he cast his eyes on my gun and looked me in the eye. There was no pleading for life, any emotion, or fear. The bag fell over his face, resting on his shoulders. I wondered about his final thoughts, this close to death.

"It was my turn. I could feel everyone's eyes on me. Shorty and Slim stepped back as I moved to the detective's right side. There was movement behind me. I turned and saw the men and boys jockey for position to see the execution. It was like a cowboy movie back home, where the whole town shows up to

Aug 12, 1945

Forgot to mention, on the 10th the details of the shooting that took place at camp. Cliff stated that everybody in the camp assisted him in the execution. Slim gave Cliff the .45 and the OK sign and then proceeded in tying the detective. Several men went across the log and started to dig the grave before the man was even tied — Blood thirsty characters. The Chinese asked him if he had anything to say and he said "No" if he had to die — that's life. These people value life like a plug nickel. Fantastic. Well Cliff shot him in the head, but he didn't die immediately so Cliff fired another shot into his heart. This disturbed Cliff a little, but he didn't realize that the fellow was already unconscious and that the heart would naturally keep pumping blood for a short time. He was buried and most of his belongings were confiscated by the men in camp. Cliff himself got a wicker basket and shirt out of the deal.

Duffy's diary entry detailing the Jap detective's execution

witness the hanging of the bad guy. I think most of them saw the shooting as entertaining.

"The whole thing seemed to last forever and I wanted to put it behind me. I released the safety on the .45 and pulled the hammer back until it clicked. The Jap detective flinched and tensed his body with the sound. I pointed the barrel at the spot I thought his right ear would be under the burlap, and touched the trigger. My finger lingered on the metal as I took a deep breath and exhaled. My heart raced, my palms were sweaty, and my throat swelled. I was wet from the rain, but now I noticed perspiration under my shirt and pants. Second thoughts crossed my mind, so I pulled the trigger before they gained any momentum.

"The explosion jerked the detective's head. Blood and tissue sprayed from where the bullet exited the burlap, and his body slumped against the rope around his chest. I stepped in front of him and pressed my hand to his heart and felt a beat. I stepped back and pointed the gun at his chest and pulled the trigger. The explosion caused me to blink. When I looked, there was a small black hole, but little blood and his body lay limp. I searched for the heartbeat, but it was gone. He was dead.

"The Chinese drew closer to inspect the body. One pulled the head up to see the bullet's exit wound, revealing shredded burlap, soaked in blood. I took my knife, cut the rope, and the body fell in a heap.

"Shorty, Slim, and two others lifted the man and walked to the shallow grave and dropped him in. The burlap fell from his head and was tossed into the hole, but with his head exposed, the men and boys were pointing and jabbering over the wounds. While they threw dirt on the Jap detective's face and chest, I turned away and headed back across the stream to our camp. I had seen enough."

"Did it upset you?" I asked.

"This may sound callous, Duff, but I didn't feel remorseful or sick over killing him. It did bother me that his heart was still pumping."

"Saltz, the man was dead with the shot to the head. His heart would naturally keep pumping blood for a short time, but he was already gone."

"I guess so."

"We split up his possessions and I chose the wicker basket and a shirt. I can't look at the basket without recalling his last moments. The shirt I'm wearing is his. When I first put it on, a chill raced down my spine . . . I imagine it will wear off with time. You know, I feel worse about claiming his possessions than I do about killing him."

I didn't care to hear anymore. The thought of the Jap detective's possessions whirled in my head. *Wicker basket, two shirts, pair shorts, toothbrush, hair comb, tin cup and broken eyeglasses. Not much to show for a man's life.*

Saltz and Bussey got fried on brandy and argued throughout the evening. Again, due to stomach pain, I refrained from the brandy and turned in early. I was plenty disgusted with the entire situation. What a display for these people to see.

I hate this war. . . .

Japan Surrenders

B ussey, Saltz and I sat around Yiok's teak table drawing up plans for the days ahead, with Khaki, Yapper and Angry standing guard outside.

During a break we tuned in the portable receiver and picked up, *"President Truman has announced the secret development of the greatest scientific advance of all time. A great bomb—an atomic bomb—dropped by the Americans August 6 on Hiroshima, Japan, estimated to have destroyed sixty percent of the city."*

"Sixty percent of Hiroshima!" I said. "Can you imagine the force of that bomb? This will bring the Japs to their knees!"

"I find it hard to believe they'll quit. Their mentality has been, 'Fight to the last man and die with honor.'" Bussey said.

"Die with honor—what nonsense. They're pawns of Hirohito and his military," I said.

Next, we heard that Russia had declared war on Japan.

Sure, now 'Uncle Joe Stalin' will join us to defeat the Japanese Empire. What a phony! You can bet Stalin is looking to prosper by hopping on board for the ride into Tokyo. He probably wants Manchuria for starters. He worries me. Their tentacles reach all the way to Malaya and Singapore. Communism will be our next threat once the war is over.

The following day—August 9—the news was broadcast that America had dropped a second atomic bomb on the city of Nagasaki and the Russians were marching on Manchuria. News was breaking so quickly that it left little time for me to comprehend I could be going home soon, to Peggy and the children.

The end for the "Land of the Rising Sun" was near. It was about time the sun set over Japan!

August 11, 1945—The announcement came:

"THE JAPANESE HAVE ASKED FOR PEACE!"

Holy bedlam broke loose! We stood by the whole day, nervous wrecks, but the definitive terms of surrender didn't come. Seven months to the day since we parachuted into Malaya. I knew something would happen, but not this development—Happy Days!

I broke down. Tears of joy, happiness, and a release of the fear and anxiety I had shoved aside to remain firm in my determination to survive, to go home to Peggy.

Faith was all I had had to lean on for seven months, and many days I believed I would die and—like Carl—be buried in a shallow grave in Malaya's jungle.

Now, I envisioned my arms wrapped around that

beautiful redhead—my passion queen, Margaret Mary Therese McCormick Duffy. I hadn't hugged and kissed Peggy for over a year and a half . . . we had some catching up to do.

I'm coming home, Red!

I wondered if our son, Danny, would remember me and if our daughter Peggy Anne would let me—a stranger to her—hug, kiss, and smell her powdered skin. My daughter was nearly one year old, and I had yet to hold her in my arms and kiss her cheek or tiny fingers.

Thoughts were whirling through my head, with peace at hand. The joy and excitement was electrifying, and we danced and hugged, and danced again.

Our celebration was interrupted when a Chinese coolie—flanked by Bussey's boys—burst into the room.

"We have visitors!" Yiok said. "Quick, hide at Number 24 house, while I tend to them."

"The war's over, Yiok!" Saltz said.

"The Japs might not think so," I said.

"Please, go to Number 24 house. Do not make trouble!"

Bussey took charge. "Duff, grab the receiver. Saltz, the map and plans. Angry and Khaki, protect our rear and, Yapper, work your way around their side and get a good look at them. If we don't hear from you in fifteen minutes, we'll head to camp."

In seconds we cleared out, hustling to Number 24 house, last plantation quarters before the jungle.

Once inside, Saltz, Bussey and I stood guard at three open-air windows at the front of the building. Angry was at the front door and Khaki at the rear, where we could easily slip out and escape into the jungle.

The building was one room and resembled an army barracks without beds—just sleeping mats and blankets tossed on a wood floor. Kerosene lamps hung by string from center posts supporting a grass roof, and insects, spiders, or snakes could come and go as they pleased. It was damp and humid—as all our shelters had been—and the odor of musty air filled our nostrils and seeped into our clothes.

Minutes passed when Yapper called out—before showing his face—to avoid startling us and drawing our gunfire.

"It's okay, no problem, we are safe! It is Yiok's brother, Kiat, from Kuala Lumpur."

We left Number 24, made our way back to Yiok's house and were introduced to our long-awaited host and owner of the plantation, the richest man in Malaya.

"Gentlemen, this is my brother Ng Teong Kiat," Yiok said.

"It's a pleasure to meet you, Kiat," I said.

"Yes, nice to meet you," Saltz added.

He reminded me of a Southern gentleman, with his white Panama suit and shoes, and his warm smile. He removed his matching hat, exposing a head of salt and pepper hair, slicked with tonic.

He wasn't as heavy as I had envisioned. He was gracious in his manner and spoke excellent English.

Saltz and I traded bows with him, while Bussey wrapped his arms around the wide man.

"Hello, Kiat," Bussey said. "We've been waiting for you. What took you so damn long?"

"It has been difficult to leave Kuala Lumpur. The Japanese have kept a close watch on me and other business leaders. Their high command claimed it was for our own safety, saying guerrillas have been ambushing motorcars and taking hostages. But I believe they have formed a Japanese death squad to murder our leaders before the Allies land in Malaya."

"But the war is over, Kiat!" Bussey said.

"I will not feel safe until Malaya is liberated. Until then, I wish to hide at your camp, Captain Bussey."

"Sure, Kiat, we'll leave at sunrise."

Kiat turned to Saltz and me, and said, "I hope my brother has been able to make your stay comfortable, gentlemen."

"Yiok has been wonderful," Saltz said. "And we're grateful for your help too, Kiat."

"Yes, thank you very much," I said. "Since we arrived we have eaten well. Before, we were lucky if we had a handful of rice."

"I am sorry for the difficulty living in the jungle has brought upon you, but this shall come to an end soon."

"Yes, very soon we hope." I said.

We dined, shared our tale with Kiat, and celebrated Japan asking for peace, all the while waiting and listening for the announcement from our Allied leaders.

Four and one half hours sleep, up at 0330 and got ready to escort Kiat and Big Son into camp. Nearly a dozen in our party, with all the foodstuffs and gear. The old boy did quite well, considering his size, the difficulty of the trail, and all the climbing. But he'll need to replace his white suit.

At 1815, I was listening to Manila broadcasting and the official surrender of Japan came through. This was 45 minutes after the announcement by the Emperor of Japan. Troops were to surrender and lay down their arms in all occupied areas and President Truman would speak in a few hours. General MacArthur—Supreme Commander in the Pacific—was appointed as Head of the Allied Occupation Forces and he immediately dispatched instructions to Tokyo.

Things went hog wild in camp. Wine, whiskey and duck made up our feast's menu, with Bussey shooting the M-3 in a victory volley. Much gambling and happiness surround us, and I get very tired and sentimental for Peg, the little ones and home. It won't be hard to spend this Christmas at home.

Peace at last!

"Let's go back to the plantation and wait for instructions from the Second Detachment," Bussey said the next morning.

That's all it took for Saltz and me to make our decision. We were tired of jungle life.

"Kiat, we're going back to the plantation. What would you like to do?" Bussey asked.

"I wish to stay here. I am afraid the Japs will come for me."

"Okay. Slim is at your service if you need anything. Sleep in our quarters, that will give you your privacy."

"Thank you, Captain. Please, keep silent of my whereabouts."

It was early evening when our party returned to the plantation and Yiok's house. He fed us—Bussey, his three boys, Saltz, Big Son and me—and we turned in for the night at Number 24 house.

The next two days we monitored the radio receiver, anxious for news of Allied Forces landing in Malaya or a report from Second Detachment. Time dragged on as we waited.

On August 17, at 1300, Khaki was on surveillance when he rushed into Yiok's dining room and announced, "There is a Jap high officer on a Harley-Davidson at the plantation office. He's wearing a saber, and puttees wrap his legs!"

"How many are with him?" Bussey asked.

"He's alone."

"Let's grab him! He'll be a good source of information and I'd like that saber for a souvenir," Bussey said.

"Khaki, hustle down by bicycle and nab him, while the rest of us come in on the footpath behind the office."

"Captain, do not cause any trouble. Let the Jap officer be!" Yiok pleaded.

"Don't worry, Yiok, everything will be fine," Bussey said.

"This is not a good idea!" Yiok said.

Khaki took off, pedaling toward the office. Coming in on the footpath were Bussey, Saltz, Angry, Yapper, Yiok, Big Son and me.

We reached the back entrance of the office, leading into a kitchen. Beyond was Yiok's private office and at the front were a larger office, reception area, and the front door. Standing outside on the U-shaped drive was Khaki.

"The Jap officer was gone before I arrived."

"Damn!" Bussey said. "Let's wait inside to see if any other Jap officers show up."

"Bussey, what are we going to accomplish by taking a Jap?" I asked.

"We can gather information about their leaders and headquarters, take them prisoner."

"For what purpose? It's not worth the risk of getting ourselves shot."

We were debating our next step when a motorcar pulled up to the building.

"Let's take this car," Bussey said. The next moment, Bussey's boys dashed out the door, surrounded the car and pointed their guns in the open windows. Three Chinese—a man and two teenage boys—occupied the car.

"Out of the car and put your hands on top of your head!" Bussey ordered.

The three were escorted into the front office, tied up and taken to the kitchen. Meanwhile, Yapper drove the car to a secluded place, out of sight of passing traffic.

"Captain Bussey, this is Dr. Chong Loke. He is resident doctor of Kuantan, and the boys are his sons," Yiok said.

Dr. Loke's wallet held a card identifying him as a doctor and President of the Overseas Chinese Association for Malaya. The association's members were sympathetic to homeland China and its people, contributing financial aid to help combat the Second Sino-Japanese War, which began in 1937 when Japan invaded China. The Jap attack on Pearl Harbor merged their war with World War II.

"Captain, two more motorcars have arrived!"

Khaki hollered from the front office.

"Yapper, take Dr. Loke and his boys to the manager's house and wait until you hear from me," Bussey ordered. "The rest of you come with me."

Bussey, Saltz, Big Son and I hurried to join Khaki and Angry.

"Captain, please stop before you go too far!" Yiok begged, as he trailed us to the front office.

Two Aston Martin motorcars were stopped on the drive and its occupants, all Malay gentlemen with little gray beards, piled out. A 1940 baby blue Packard carrying three more men pulled in behind the Astons.

"Let's take them!" Bussey yelled.

Out we dash and surround ten or twelve distinguished-looking Malays. From the Packard stepped a good-sized man wearing blue silk pants, yellow shirt, embroidered jacket, and pink silk slippers.

"Captain, this is the Sultan of Pahang, Tengku Abu Bakar," Yiok said.

"Who are the rest of the men?" Bussey asked.

"They are officials of the State of Pahang."

"Duff, move these boys to the kitchen. Saltz, Big Son, and I will ditch the cars around back. Angry and Khaki, stay here at the front door and keep an eye on the road," Bussey said.

Back in the kitchen, Yiok and I had our hands full with all the people rounded up. I had an exchange of words with the Sultan and his party and realized we had gone too far in this hair-raising scheme of Bussey's.

One man was the district officer of Kuantan, one acting district officer of Pekan, several were clerks and secretaries, one was an Indian Public Works Department official. The Sultan's residence was in Pekan.

The Sultan had served for eleven years under the British, had three wives, nine children, and was quite a horseman. His royal robes made him a very fashionable figure. *Oh, for the life of a Sultan!*

Bussey, Saltz and Big Son entered through the backdoor and had concocted a story about how we were here to protect the Sultan and his cabinet from the Japs. Yiok stood by wringing his hands.

The Sultan was quite surprised that Americans had come to protect him, but it put him at ease. He admitted he was nervous about the Japs and his safety, now that he wasn't needed to keep control of the people in the state of Pahang, as expected by the Japs during the occupation.

Khaki burst into the kitchen, getting everyone's attention and blurted out, "A lorry has pulled in the drive loaded with Japs!"

"Khaki, get up there and grab Angry! Have him drop back and don't let the Japs see you," I said. "Bussey, we need to get these people out of here!"

Up front, Angry started yelling and then a terrific volley of gunfire filled the air, followed by an extremely loud explosion, which shook the building.

"Quick, everyone out of here!" Bussey yelled.

The kitchen emptied outside. Yiok and Big Son led the Sultan and his men into the brush, disappearing into the thick foliage.

My heart raced, while Bussey, Saltz and I pulled together a plan.

"I'll push around the south side of the building to the front," I said. "Who wants the north side?"

"I'll take it," Saltz said.

"Bussey, that leaves you to enter the kitchen and make your way to the front office. You okay with that?"

"No, but I'm on my way."

Not sure what was in store the next few minutes worried me. I hugged the outside wall, silently stepping my way to the front of the building.

Angry was yelling in Chinese and more shots rang out. I had a .45 revolver drawn, but didn't feel too secure as I approached the corner of the building, where the drive led back to the road.

I poked my head out as the Jap lorry whined its gears and shot out the drive, escaping south on the motor road. Two dozen Jap soldiers fled on foot behind it.

I fired a few rounds at the Jap troops, as did our other men, but missed.

"Angry, Khaki, hold your fire! This is Duffy on your right. Saltz is coming up on your left and Bussey through the office. What's the situation?"

"It's clear—the last of them are gone," Khaki hollered.

"Hold your fire, I'm coming out," Saltz yelled.

Stepping around the corner I saw Angry, Khaki and Bussey at the front door. I scanned the area for stragglers. On the drive were the bodies of four Jap soldiers.

Lying just inside the office door was a Jap officer. He had a half-dozen holes in his back and his shirt was soaked with blood.

"What the hell happened?" Bussey asked his boys.

"The Jap lorry pulled in, stopped, and this Jap officer jumped from the truck and started in the front door." Angry said.

"I was at the doorway to the hall when he spotted me and turned to run. I shouted to stop or I would shoot. He didn't stop, so I unloaded my carbine and dropped him.

"I made my way to the door and saw about thirty Japs! Most had gotten off the lorry, so I pulled the pin on a grenade, tossed it and dove for cover.

"After the explosion, Khaki arrived and we let out a few more rounds, trying to hit the Japs as they fled. That's when you arrived."

Yiok had pleaded with Bussey numerous times, but he didn't listen or take him seriously. I could kick myself for not putting a stop to Bussey's little scheme. God only knows where this would lead.

"We need to hide the bodies and clean up this mess before anyone else shows up," Bussey said.

"Khaki, grab a couple coolies and bury the Japs out back. Angry, get over to the manager's house and tell Yapper to escort the doctor and his boys to Number 24 house. Warn the manager and his wife that there could be trouble and to put the word out to the plantation workers. We'll all meet at Number 24!"

We rounded up Yiok, Big Son, and the Sultan and his gang, and headed for cover.

Reaching Number 24, we tried to organize things best we could—men, women, children, cripples, everybody was pouring into the place—what a convention!

Word had got out about our skirmish with the Japs and they all knew trouble was coming and wanted protection. More arrived every hour.

Shortly before nightfall we dispatched two runners

to Second Detachment. Our boys were instructed to travel through the night. The note spelled out the mess we were in and asked Hump and the British for help. We hadn't a clue what they could do, but we had to try something.

"Duff, let's get the cars at the office and ditch them, so the Japs don't get their hands on them." Bussey said. "Saltz, take charge while we're gone. I'll leave Khaki to give a hand."

"Go ahead, we'll mind the store," Saltz said.

About 1900 we started down the wood potato trail making our way to the office. Halfway, we heard a rustling in the brush and saw the flames of torches approaching.

"Bussey, we got company," I whispered.

Our group slid into the bushes and took cover. We put about ten feet between the trail and us. Bussey had his tommy gun, I carried a carbine, and we each had one hand grenade and a sidearm.

The torches cast their light on our position as the party neared, walking single file. I figured the Japs had come. My heart raced and I could hardly swallow.

In the lead were a few Chinese, followed by a dozen Japs with their hands bound in rope. Behind the last of them was Yapper with a .45 revolver in one hand and a halter connecting his prisoners in the other.

Bussey and I looked at one another in shock.

Behind Yapper were several more Chinese villagers, Dr. Loke, and his two sons.

"Yapper, it's Bussey, hold up!"

"Oh, Captain, you scared me!" Yapper said, pointing his gun back at the Japs.

Yapper's prisoners were all Malays in Jap uniforms. It was common for the Japs to force Malays to serve under them—or suffer hardship, and death. Naturally, their own people treated them as traitors.

"What's going on?" Bussey asked.

"I was in the village when all these Japs came running down the motor road. I caught half, but the others got away. I might have got the truck too, if my carbine was loaded."

"Good work, Yap. You should get a medal."

"It was easy—they ran to me. All I did was point my .45 and holler, 'Stop!' I had one more but he was wounded badly. There was nothing I could do for him, so I shot him dead."

It was a remarkable sight, Yapper and a dozen prisoners gift wrapped. We escorted Yapper and the prisoners to Number 24, and set out again.

At the office, we put drivers behind the wheels of the Sultan's Packard, Dr. Loke's car, and the two Astons. We ditched them deep in the plantation and camouflaged them with brush.

Returning to Number 24, we found the place in turmoil. Nearly the whole village was there! We tried to get some rest but it was no use.

Early the next morning we sent 140 men and women, 50 children, the Sultan and his party, Mr. Wong's family, Mr. Chu's family, and Big Son to Bussey's camp for safekeeping. We had to protect these people from the Japs.

This left Bussey, his three boys, Saltz, me, and fifteen of our best men making up our garrison at Number 24.

We posted guards a quarter mile out on every trail leading to our hideout and sent scouts every few hours to size up the Jap situation.

August 18, 1945—Sat around and waited to see what developed. Nothing occurred, but our scouts told us plenty of Japs had arrived at the office and they were trying to catch coolies and had fired shots several times. A few were injured and killed during the shooting.

August 19, 1945—Hanging on the radio waiting for announcement telling us occupation forces were on their way to Malaya, but all we got was delays and more delays. The emissaries to Manila didn't arrive (something about the coloring of the airplane they were to use). Fighting still going on in some sectors and things were generally snafu.

More Japs arrived at the office and more shooting in the village—Number 24 is packed with people now. We must have at least 200 people on our hands. . . . It's very tense and everyone is on edge. All we can do is wait—sleep is hard to get.

It was the third day when a runner returned with a message from Second Detachment. He had lost his companion in the vicinity of Jerantut and bicycled over one hundred miles since setting out on our mission.

He was captured by the Japs and questioned as to whether he was working with Allied soldiers. He claimed he was "just a paddy field worker"! They didn't believe him, but they let him go.

The man was a physical and mental wreck. We put him under the care of Dr. Loke, hoping he could calm the man.

August 22, 1945—Third wedding anniversary and

I'm farther from Peg now than anytime I've been in Malaya. If we get out of this scrape it will be a miracle, but by no means have I given up hope. I'll be home for Christmas, Peg, that's a promise. All my love, darling!

British Admiral Lord Louis Mountbatten is sending communiqués to the Commander of the Southern Armies, trying to make arrangements for the end of hostilities and for the landing of Allied troops in Malaya and other points. I hope to hell he gets some results!

Japs are still firing scattered shots throughout the village and about 200 Jap soldiers have now set up headquarters at the plantation office. Waiting and trying to keep our wits about us under the circumstances.

August 23, 1945—Seven trucks reported at the office and shots ring out occasionally.

Our runner, who took the message to the Second Detachment, has gone crazy and we had to tie him up the last two days. He attacked Bussey. Yapper had to hit and choke him into submission. He then went after Mr. Wong, trying to bite him and grabbing him around the waist. It took three of us to pull him off. He was strong as an ox. Finally restrained him after our cook gave him one hell of a kick to the chest.

While this went on, a scream came from out back of Number 24 and everyone started running. Out we bolt and learn one of our boys slit his throat and was bleeding to death! Dr. Loke stopped the bleeding by having him drink limejuice. Doc said the calcium in the lime does the trick. The fellow had some leaves stuffed in his pockets and told the men this was his medicine. He said to put these on his neck and it would heal the wound. Funny, this guy gathered the leaves to treat himself before slitting his throat!

August 24, 1945—The Japs told the Chinese and Indians in the village, that they won't cause any trouble as long as they don't run away or act suspicious. They claim all they want is to locate four Europeans. I wonder where they obtained that information!

Crazy man is crazier and is getting on everybody's nerves. Herbs fail to mend his mental state and he continues to run around nude, playing with his privates. He remains tied in the chicken house and slips out of his bonds every so often and makes a dash for freedom—very sad. The throat slitter is getting better.

Had an exam by the Doc and he said I had internal injuries from when I bailed out, but claims a further examination is really necessary. He stated I would probably have pains for the next forty years if I don't receive treatment.

Six more days passed. It appeared the Japs were nervous about combing the jungle, for fear of an ambush. Lucky for us, because we were outnumbered and lacked weapons and ammunitions to go around. Our boys, though sympathetic to Malaya, lacked any training and experience to fight the hateful Japs.

I was scared.

I had fought almost eight months to survive, and the war was over, yet the fighting continued. If only we could hold on until the formal surrender papers were signed and Allied troops occupied Malaya. . . .

Dear God, please protect us during these desperate hours and return us to our loved ones.

On August 30, we made a trip to our jungle camp to report on activities in the village and boost morale.

The Sultan, his boys, and the millionaire brother

Kiat were pleased with the arrangements despite coping with snakes, insects, rain, poor hygiene, little food, and limited sleeping quarters. They were just grateful to be alive and protected from the Japs, and the fight we likely faced.

Before returning to Number 24, I suggested exchanging names and addresses, in the event we didn't see each other again.

The district officer of Kuantan, Dato Mohammad bin Mat—sporting a two hundred year-old knife in his belt—took charge of the exchange. The man's travels had taken him around the globe and a more cultured, educated man would be hard to find in Malaya. Afterward, good friends separated and we returned to our plantation fortress.

The following day, after Bussey and I returned from reconnaissance, Saltz reported what he heard while monitoring the receiver.

"Good news!"

"What have you got?" I asked.

"General MacArthur and American troops are in Tokyo, and three hundred airplanes arrive each day carrying men and supplies!

"And get this . . . fleets are off Malaya and at the head of the Malacca Straits waiting to land. They've dropped medical supplies and personnel into Singapore. The only delay to complete occupation is the formal signing of the treaty in the Yokohama area of Japan, on September 2."

Holed up in Number 24, we discussed the wonderful news and speculated on the days ahead. It was hard to believe the end was near, after battling to survive the past eight months. It didn't seem real.

Nonetheless, we were to face two hundred Japs at the plantation office.

"Japs! The Japs are coming!" Khaki yelled, as he charged into Number 24.

"Where are they?" Bussey asked.

"They're coming up the wood potato trail."

"How much time do we have?"

"None."

"Bussey, let's get the hell out of here!" I said.

"Yeah, let's duck in the jungle," Saltz said. "Its too big a risk—we're safer in the bush."

We hadn't even settled on our plan when a dozen of our boys ran out the door and hightailed into the jungle. This left the three of us, and Angry, Yapper, Khaki, the crazy man and the throat slitter.

"Okay, let's run!" Bussey said. "Duff, get the receiver, everyone else grab the weapons and supplies, and head out the back on the double!"

"What about the crazy man and the throat slitter?" I asked.

"Set the crazy man free! Maybe he'll follow us, but we can't be wrestling with him—not with the Japs on our tail. The throat slitter can't be moved, so he stays. He's better off here."

I cut the ropes holding the crazy man and he dashed out the back door and actually ran in the right direction.

"The Japs are here!" Yapper called.

I glanced out a window and spotted a large non-commissioned officer within thirty feet of our building. Behind him other Japs followed. Each carried a rifle.

Bussey, Saltz, and I spread out and each took a window. Angry and Yapper stood on either side of the front door and Khaki joined Bussey.

"Let them make the first move," I said.

Five more Japs followed the officer into the small clearing. We cocked our guns.

Behind the last of the Japs came four white men. I couldn't believe my eyes. It didn't make sense.

"Hey, hold your fire . . . don't shoot . . . it's me, Hump!"

"It's Humphrey!" I said.

"What the hell is going on?" Saltz asked.

"Keep your guns on the Japs," Bussey ordered.

We kept watch as the Japs stopped ten feet short of us. Hump continued past them and stopped short of the door.

"Hey, you dopes, don't you know the war's over?" Hump asked, smiling.

We held our ground while Hump explained, keeping our eyes on the six Jap soldiers standing before us.

"Relax, guys, we've come to get you out of this fix! We've arranged safe passage to Second Detachment and these boys are here to insure our safety."

I couldn't believe it—face-to-face with the enemy and Hump to boot—it didn't make sense. Not after months of evading the Japs, while fighting to survive. Now they were escorts?

"Second Detachment met with Jap officials at Jerantut and negotiated a truce to put an end to hostilities here at the plantation. In return, Second Detachment is to use their influence in getting the

Communist guerrillas to settle down," Hump explained. Accompanying Hump were Major Leonard, Captain Robinson, and Captain Dorrety—British and Australian officers.

"Pack up, guys, we want to get out of here on the double," Hump said. "With all the Japs swarming the area, we want to be at camp before nightfall."

We made our way to Yiok's home and shared an emotional goodbye. The man's love, kindness, and generosity the past two months had assured our survival at the risk of his own life.

"Yiok, thank you for everything." I said.

"It was an honor and my duty to help."

"Thank you, Yiok." Saltz said. "Sure enjoyed our time together and the brandy was great."

"Please, take a case and share it with the men of the Second Detachment."

"Perhaps we will meet again, Yiok, maybe in America. It would be my pleasure to welcome you in my home," I said.

"Yes, I hope we meet again."

"Me too, Yiok," Hump said. "Thank you."

"Yiok, buddy, I'll miss you," Bussey said, as he wrapped his arms around the man.

"Captain Bussey, it has been both interesting and a pleasure to be in your company. I will never forget you, my friend."

"Thank you, Yiok."

We got the Sultan's Packard, which had a flat tire, and pushed it to the plantation office. There we faced two hundred Jap troops and the Jap officer in charge of the whole state of Pahang.

They were shocked to see just Bussey, Saltz, and me and probably disappointed they hadn't attempted to wipe us out. They were tough looking and any minute you expected a bayonet through your back or a bullet from one of their rifles. I'll never forget how efficient and competent they appeared, and how they cooperated with us—it surprised us all.

We borrowed a Jap tire pump and changed the wheel on the Packard while the Japs watched. Our nerves were on edge as we wrestled with the wrench and lug nuts.

With the tire changed, we saluted the Jap commander and made a quick exit. Leonard, Robinson, Bussey, and I boarded the Packard. Hump, Saltz, Dorrety, and Bussey's boys hopped into the back of a lorry along with our Jap escorts. It sure felt good to be sitting on a plush leather seat and riding, instead of walking, in Malaya.

Halfway into our journey the Packard quit. The battery came out of its frame and shorted against the side. The points were all burned and I imagined the Sultan would be plenty upset.

We climbed in the back of the lorry with the Japs lending a hand, while they held our carbines. Once aboard they passed our weapons back to us and offered us cigarettes. It was unbelievable!

I saw a side to the Japs my thoughts hadn't entertained. In the eyes of one, I sensed he too was tired of war and just wanted to go home. Still, I was uneasy with showing any faith or trust. I wasn't about to forget or lay aside my prejudices because the surrender had taken place. No, I kept up my guard—they were the same

enemy responsible for rape, torture, and vicious acts
of brutality and murder throughout the Pacific and
Southeast Asia for nearly four years, and China for
fifteen years! They would have to answer for their
savage behavior against humanity.

The road north carried several Jap convoys, which
detained us many times. Upon ferrying across the
Pahang River we were received by a twenty minute egg
Jap officer, who invited us to have coffee. We were
escorted to the coffee shop by armed guards with fixed
bayonets!

The Jap was a quite a character. We had three
cups of coffee and listened—through an interpreter—
how the guerrillas had shot him in the arm. He thought
the guerrillas were a big farce and completely ignored
his injury.

Finally, he allowed us to continue our journey and
we arrived at the Jerantut Estate, where the British and
Australians had recently moved their headquarters,
and we bedded down for the night. It was a beautiful
feeling to be free of the danger we had faced merely
hours ago!

*September 2, 1945—Well, the Peace Treaty has been
signed in Yokohama harbor aboard the USS Missouri.
General MacArthur presided, General Wainwright
(forced to surrender in 1942 at Corregidor) received one
of the pens and Sir Percival (Commander of Singapore
when it fell) another. Damn glad they got it on paper!*

*About 2000, who should arrive here but Lt. Col.
Frederick Spencer Chapman, British officer who was in
Malaya during most of the occupation period. He had
only departed from here four months ago by submarine*

and parachuted back in two days ago. He certainly lived up to the reports we had on him and he impressed one as being a regular Joe. Told us of some of his experiences living with the guerrillas and trouble with the Japs—he had been captured twice by the Japs and escaped both times! A more interesting career I've never heard and he certainly looks the part. He bunked with me and we compared notes for about a half hour before falling off to sleep. An evening I'll remember a long time!

"A message was radioed from OSS. You're to proceed immediately to Singapore," Bussey said to Hump, Saltz and me.

"What about you, Bussey?" Hump asked.

"I'm to be there by October 15. This is where we part. I'll miss you boys."

"Sorry you're not coming with us, Bussey," Hump said.

"Yeah, me too. Give me your addresses so I can look you up when I get back to the States," Bussey said.

"We're grateful to you, Bussey!" I said. "If not for you and Yiok, our last two months would have been miserable."

"You're a character, Bussey, I'll say that for you!" Saltz said.

"Well, I try. . . ."

"No hard feelings?" Bussey said, looking at each of us.

"No hard feelings." Saltz said.

We parted good friends and began our journey by motorcar up to Kuala Lipis, where we ran into twelve hundred Japs. They appeared arrogant and indifferent to the Jap surrender. They would bow and nod but you didn't want to turn your back.

An Indian doctor examined me. He believed my stomach pain was nothing to worry about, but said X-rays and observation would be necessary to determine just what was going on internally.

The three of us and our Indian driver journeyed south passing Raub and Fraser's Hill, and eventually arrived in Kuala Lumpur. We inquired of a Jap officer where to find Allied Headquarters and were politely told we were two days early!

We pushed on toward Singapore, stopping at Kampong Kota, where we had parachuted in, hoping to see our friend Talib—the man who helped us our first day in Malaya. He couldn't be found.

The local people confirmed that three of our boys died with the crash of the *Postville Express* and four were taken prisoner, but they had no news of their whereabouts. We asked them to thank Talib and bid him farewell, then parted.

North of Johore Bahru—outside of Singapore—at the ungodly hour of 0400, we met thousands of Japs camped along both sides of the road. It went on for five miles and I think I held my breath most the way. It turned out to be the entire Jap army ordered out of Singapore by the British. There were hundreds of motorcars, trucks, artillery pieces, everything imaginable lining the road. Campfires burned all over the place illuminating Jap faces, yet they ignored us as we steered our motorcar slowly past them and reached the causeway to Singapore.

We wandered the city's streets four hours looking for someone to help us until routed to Major Smith—

Route of 'Postville Express' Crew

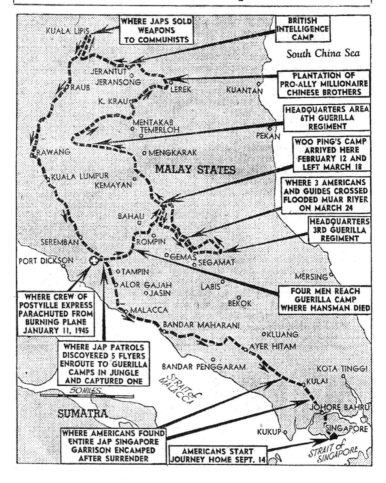

WHERE JAPS SOLD WEAPONS TO COMMUNISTS

BRITISH INTELLIGENCE CAMP

KUALA LIPIS

South China Sea

JERANTUT
JERANSONG
RAUB
LEREK
KUANTAN
K. KRAU

PLANTATION OF PRO-ALLY MILLIONAIRE CHINESE BROTHERS

HEADQUARTERS AREA 6TH GUERILLA REGIMENT

MENTAKAB
TEMERLOH
PEKAN

RAWANG
MENGKARAK
MALAY STATES

WOO PING'S CAMP ARRIVED HERE FEBRUARY 12 AND LEFT MARCH 18

KUALA LUMPUR
KEMAYAN

WHERE 3 AMERICANS AND GUIDES CROSSED FLOODED MUAR RIVER ON MARCH 24

BAHAU

HEADQUARTERS 3RD GUERILLA REGIMENT

SEREMBAN
ROMPIN
PORT DICKSON
GEMAS
SEGAMAT

MERSING

TAMPIN
ALOR GAJAH
JASIN
LABIS
BEKOK

FOUR MEN REACH GUERILLA CAMP WHERE HANSMAN DIED

WHERE CREW OF POSTVILLE EXPRESS PARACHUTED FROM BURNING PLANE JANUARY 11, 1945

MALACCA
BANDAR MAHARANI

KLUANG
AYER HITAM

WHERE JAP PATROLS DISCOVERED 5 FLYERS ENROUTE TO GUERILLA CAMPS IN JUNGLE AND CAPTURED ONE

BANDAR PENGGARAM
KOTA TINGGI
KULAI

50 MILES

STRAIT of MALACCA

SUMATRA

JOHORE BAHRU

WHERE AMERICANS FOUND ENTIRE JAP SINGAPORE GARRISON ENCAMPED AFTER SURRENDER

KUKUP
SINGAPORE

AMERICANS START JOURNEY HOME SEPT. 14

STRAIT of SINGAPORE

in charge of evacuating Americans from Singapore.

We inquired about our captured crew—Gillett, Govednik, Lindley, and MacDonald—hoping to discover their fate at the hands of the Japs. We stood by in silence, hoping for the best. I bit my lip as Smith dug through files and ledgers coming up blank each time. I prayed for good news, but feared the worst.

"Here they are!" Smith said.

"We evacuated all four of your boys eight days ago. Flew them to Calcutta and have them at the Station Hospital. You'll be going there for medical evaluation and treatment before returning to the States, so you can say hello!"

Smith took the facts of our story and escorted us to the governor's mansion where we saw plenty of rank rolling around. We stayed outside because of our ragged clothes until approached by an American general named Tunner, who asked us to join him for dinner and share our story. He stated we had Number 1 priority to be evacuated and would leave on the first plane that arrived.

A three-hour interview and photos with three war correspondents took up the evening. Then we found our quarters—Room Number 46 of the lavish Raffles Hotel, the best spot in Singapore.

The soft bed was uncomfortable, after spending eight months on sapling beds and the jungle floor. But my first shower was wonderful!

Standing beneath a stream of hot water, I took the hotel's scented soap and lathered my skin and hair, scrubbing at the jungle dirt. The dirt and grime was in my skin, so it seemed, and the skin's gray and yellow color was quite noticeable, as I stood before the bathroom mirror. Sores, cuts, and wounds—many open and infected—covered my gaunt body from head to toe. I cringed at the results of starvation and malnutrition, but mostly the deep cankerous holes the jungle leeches had left in my skin.

Studying the face in the mirror—I seldom saw it during jungle life—I dreamed of Peggy and going home, wrapping my arms around her waist, smelling her perfumed skin, kissing her soft lips. I hungered for her! It was over a year and a half since we had spoken to each other, except by letter. The crash of the *Postville Express* halted even that luxury. And Peggy had no way of knowing for the past eight months whether I was dead or alive . . . except for my promise: *"Peggy, darling, if they tell you I'm missing or dead, don't believe it, I'm coming back!"*

The next few days I wandered around Singapore and its shops, purchasing a few gifts for Peggy, but couldn't find anything for the little ones. I witnessed the formal ceremony of the Japanese surrender with Lord Louis Mountbatten presiding. It was a historic occasion.

I was proud of the job we did to save the world from the clutches of evil men with selfish ideologies and their brutal methods in carrying them out. But so many men, women and children had suffered and died before peace was in hand. So many lives were changed forever.

September 14 arrived and with it our departure in an American C-54 transport plane. Hump, Saltz and I climbed aboard and minutes later the big bird raced down the runway, gaining speed before lifting off and climbing toward a blue sky.

I peered out a small window and spotted the floating dry dock we were sent to bomb on our last mission. I was happy to see it had been smashed up badly.

I looked out over the jungle's canopy, its hills and rivers winding their way toward the sea. A morning mist hung over its lush green cover. I thought of Billings, Kundrat and Spratt, who died with the crash of the *Postville Express* on that fateful morning of 11 January 1945. It seemed so long ago. And my friend Carl Hansman, buried in a shallow grave deep in the jungle beneath the canopy I stared down on.

I reached in my pocket and pulled out my wedding band. Carefully I slid the cut ring on my finger, leaned my head against the cabin wall, and closed my eyes. . . .

HEADQUARTERS
INDIA CHINA DIVISION-AIR-TRANSPORT COMMAND
A. P. O. 192, c/o Postmaster
New York, N. Y.

Office of the Commanding General

Sept. 12, 1945
Singapore, Malaya
"Raffles Hotel"

My Darling Peg:

I always told you 'beautiful' that I would come back to you from this war and now I'm keeping my word.

Peg, this has to be very brief, but I'll give you all the details concerning my adventure, when I have you enfolded in my arms. Newspaper correspondents interviewed me last night; so you'll probably get most of the history, before I see you. The story briefly is as follows — Airplane disintegrated over Singapore Jan 11th and I parachuted to safety, in the Malayan jungles. Have lived the last 8 months with Chinese guerillas and arrived in Singapore yesterday morning. Am in the best of health and you can look forward to some heavy loving when I get home.

Near the end and havent even mentioned Pamm & Peggy Ann, what a father?? Kiss the little' ones and tell them Dad is coming home. All my love to you darling & the little ones, best regards to your folks & all our friends, as always & forever,

Yours, Bill

Capt. Bill & Peggy Duffy, and
children Peggy Anne & Danny
Reunited–October 1945

Peggy & Bill Duffy
1987

Journey Home

Forty-six years separated the September 1945 morning, when Dad climbed aboard a C-54 transport plane at Singapore, and the October 1991 afternoon when he gazed out the window of the veterans hospital, just outside Chicago. His eyes were fixed on a jet plane crossing the sky.

His fascination with aircraft never dimmed. The sight of the big birds stirred memories of the war, Southeast Asia and missions of the *Postville Express*. Malaya and struggles endured with the harsh life of the jungle: its heat, humidity, swamps, mud, hills, *bashas*, leeches, insects, flooding, disease, hunger, rain, Carl's death, the Communist guerrillas, and the Japanese enemy. His will to survive, rather than perish in the jungle, allowing him to return home to Peggy and their children.

Uncertainty showed on Dad's face. Wringing his

hands, he searched the hospital room with his eyes. He had lost his thoughts of minutes ago. I shaved his face, trimmed his hair, and helped him in the bathroom.

Reality was more evasive each day. How could he escape the clouds in his mind, fogging his memory of yesterday and today?

Pulling on an eyebrow, he examined his surroundings. Fear brought tears, as he struggled to remember what had happened and where he was.

"Dad, you're in the hospital."

Studying the blue-and-white-striped robe, cotton slippers, and bed—he understood.

Life like this is hardly worth living. Alzheimer's was taking over.

Time and again, Dad had said, "I'm going to beat this thing!"

He believed it—though unaware of the fight he was waging. His brain was being consumed, destroying his memory and concentration, stripping him of dignity.

As he struggled for a plan of action, his thoughts would fade and the course would begin again. He was at war with an enemy unseen and soon forgotten.

Seated on the bed, he rubbed his hands on the robe covering his thighs. He tensed his body and clenched the robe, turning his knuckles white. The rheumatoid arthritis inflamed his joints, but still he made fists.

Frustration and anger grew in his struggle with the horrible effects of Alzheimer's disease, as he looked for an answer.

I've always been amazed by his determination to persevere in times of difficulty. His strength and courage seldom yielded to anything he faced in life.

I handed him a picture of his twelve children. His eyes lingered on the faces as he touched them. Dad could name them—but not today! I jumped in before he tried, pausing between each name for him to catch up, as I touched each face.

"Danny . . .

Peggy Anne . . .

Diane . . .

Maureen . . .

Denise . . .

Kathleen . . .

Billy . . .

Jeanne . . .

Marianne . . .

Brian . . .

Michael . . .

Colleen . . ."

Dad stared at the photo a long time, before lowering it to his lap.

"Remember how you used to say, 'The church doesn't think your Mother and I have any rhythm'— and your answer, 'I think Peggy and I have plenty of rhythm . . . look at all these damn children!'"

Dad smiled. Calm—his eyes shifted to another picture I held.

"Tell me, Dad, who's this?"

"That's Red—my beautiful Peggy!"

I gave him Mom's picture and a shine lit those brilliant blue eyes, joined by a smile.

"You and Mom did a fine job. You've built a family of twelve children and thirty-four grandchildren!"

Had Dad not survived Malaya, there would be

"The Duffy Children"
Danny, Peggy Anne, Diane, Maureen, Denise, Kathleen,
Bill Jr., Jeanne, Marianne, Brian, Michael, & Colleen

"The Duffy Grandchildren"

only two Duffy children and six grandchildren.

Each January 11—anniversary of the *Postville Express* crash—we celebrated and thanked Dad for coming home.

Mom and Dad looked at each of us children as a gift. They shared the responsibility of guiding us and teaching us love, respect, happiness, compassion and laughter—and to put our faith and trust in God.

Their greatest gift was their love for each other. They openly hugged and kissed in our presence and today this lives on in their children and grandchildren.

I held Dad's hand as he lay on the bed and rested his head on the pillow. I watched him close his eyes, as I fought back tears, and swallowed past the lump in my throat.

"Dad, I love you," I whispered.

He opened his eyes, smiled, and said, "I love you too, Son!"

These would be our last words.

We hugged. I kissed his cheek, lips, and forehead. I caressed his hand, stroked the thin gray hair of his head, and took pleasure in the scent of his skin.

If only I could stay at Dad's side, his constant companion, helping battle his fear and confusion in moments when the Alzheimer's had him in its tight grip. I didn't want to let go!

I sat at Dad's bedside watching him sleep and gently held his hand, careful not to ignite the arthritis pain . . . and I cried. For Dad, Mom, my sisters and brothers . . . for me.

I kissed his lips and stroked his hair one more time as I stood over him, then turned and walked out the door.

Over the next four hours as I drove home to Iowa, I cried and prayed that God would take him. Our family's pain was too difficult and I wanted my father to be free of suffering.

"Take him, Lord . . . please take him home."

Five days after my visit—October 18, 1991, shortly after noon—the call came. . . .

"Billy—Dad died."

I've never felt such a range of emotions as in those early days after his death. It is not something I care to experience again soon. It is difficult to let go of yesterday and journey into tomorrow without those we love.

Dad died . . . but he defeated Alzheimer's disease and its grip, no longer to hinder thought and memory. His pain and suffering had ended.

One more time, Dad had returned home.

Today, Dad lives on in the hearts and souls of his beloved Peggy, their twelve children and thirty-four grandchildren.

In the years to come I will share his story with those who follow. This is my destiny.

Peggy Duffy flanked by
Jan & Bill Duffy, Jr.
Christmas 2000

Epilogue

In researching Dad's story I contacted the U.S. Army Central Identification Laboratory at Hickam Air Force Base, Hawaii. CILHI is responsible for the search, recovery, and identification of all deceased U.S. servicemen and women. I received the following report in my search for information about the remains of Lt. Col. Robinson Billings, Capt. Carl A. Hansman, T. Sgt. Michael A. Kundrat, and S. Sgt. Rouhier E. Spratt:

"According to the Unknown X-609 file, the remains of Lt. Col. Billings and T/Sgt. Kundrat were recovered from graves near the wreckage of the B-29. Lt. Col. Billings' remains returned home on 16 June 1948. Unfortunately we have not received Kundrat's individual Deceased Personnel File to provide you with the information on the date his remains were returned home.

"S/Sgt. Spratt was recovered by 61st British Graves

Registration Unit and placed in the custody of the Search and Recovery Team. His remains were interred in the National Memorial Cemetery of the Pacific on 30 September 1948."

- *Lt. Col. Robinson Billings*
  buried in Massachusetts
- *T/Sgt. Michael A. Kundrat*
  buried in Pennsylvania
- *S/Sgt. Rouhier E. Spratt*
  buried in Hawaii

"Capt. Carl A. Hansman was born on 18 July 1916. His home address was Los Angeles, Ca. At the time of the incident, his sister was the only living relative he had, who also lived in California. I am unable to disclose her name under the Privacy Act.

"According to the Unknown X-609 file, in February 1947 American Graves Registration sent a Search and Recovery team to recover the remains associated with the unaccounted for crew from this B-29. But because of complications with the Chinese guerrillas, they were unsuccessful with their attempt. Another team was sent out again in May of 1947. The following is an excerpt from the team's report:

"After a trek of over one and one half hours in which we calculated we covered about three miles we came on a grave situated about 10 feet off the East side of the trail. We excavated the grave about 2 feet wide, 6 feet long and 4 feet deep and found a partial skull (no lower jaw or no teeth), a few rib bones, a few vertebrae, some hair and two imitation pearl buttons. No identification tags or other means of identification could be found. Even before we commenced digging it was apparent that the grave had

been recently dug and looked two months old.

"Unknown X-609 was recovered from the area in which the decedent was reported buried. However, attempts to associate the unknown with Hansman were negative.

"According to the information within (Capt. Carl) Hansman's 293 file, he is still unaccounted for."

Rae Phillips
Senior Casualty Data/WWII Analyst
U.S. Army Central Identification Laboratory
Hickam Air Force Base, Hawaii
15 August 2000

Carl Hansman's remains lie in a shallow grave deep in the jungle of what was known as Malaya. But Hansman is not alone, at least not anymore.

Recently, I telephoned the homes of the remaining survivors of the *Postville Express* crew. I called Ralph Lindley, Dana Gillett, Don Humphrey, and Marty Govednik, in that order, to announce the publishing of *Destiny Ours*. I include these conversations as a tribute to these fine men.

<u>M. Sgt. Ralph Lindley</u>

Betty, Ralph's wife, answered my call. Betty and I were enjoying our conversation, when I asked, "Betty, is Ralph still alive?" Betty replied, "No, Ralph died December 26, 1992." She said his health failed as he battled various ailments, including liver disease.

Ralph—born on June 21, 1913—was seventy-nine years old. Ralph and Betty spent their lives in the small Iowa community of Onawa, not too far from the shores of the Missouri River and about an hour north of Omaha. Betty shared pieces of Ralph's life after Malaya and some details of his time as a prisoner of war.

"Ralph had nightmares all his life after his experience in the Outram Road Prison at Singapore," she said. "The Japanese beat and starved him for eight months. When he was captured he weighed 210 pounds . . . when he was liberated he weighed 86 pounds, with internal injuries from starvation, malnutrition, malaria, and the beatings he received. He never fully recovered from the experience, but over the years the nightmares he endured lessened, but always remained."

Ralph owned and operated a candy and tobacco route after Malaya and before he retired. He and Betty raised three daughters in the years after the war.

It was humorous to hear Betty share the rivalry she and Ralph enjoyed. Ralph was a St. Louis Cardinals fan and Betty a diehard Chicago Cubs fan. It seems that Betty enjoyed the jabs and heckling between them over the Cardinals and Cubs–more than the outcome of the games.

Funny that it's the little things that bind our lives and make us who and what we are.

<u>M. Sgt. Harold "Dana" Gillett</u>

Dana's wife, another Betty, answered the telephone. I was enjoying the company of my second Betty in as many hours when I finally asked, "Betty, is Dana alive?" Betty answered, "No, Dana died back on January 25, 1988." Dana was seventy-two years old. Betty said he suffered terribly from emphysema and congestive heart failure near the end of his life.

In the years after Malaya, Dana and Betty shared a life in Douglas, Ariz., having moved from their

hometown of Binghamton, N.Y. for Betty's health.
Here they raised two daughters while they owned and
operated a commercial air conditioning and refrigera-
tion business for thirty-two years. In 1986 they moved
to Tucson, closer to their daughters, where Betty
lives today.

When the *Postville Express* broke apart and debris
filled the sky, Dana was badly burned and lost part of
his ear. For the next five days he and Marty Govednik
hid out, but couldn't get across the railroad tracks the
other crew members struggled with that first day.
Dana and Marty were captured by the Japanese and
thrown in the same prison as Lindley, at Singapore.

Betty Gillett shared stories similar to Betty
Lindley's: "Dana had nightmares all his life after
spending eight months as a prisoner of war. The
Japanese beat the men any time they were caught
speaking to one another. Dana weighed 160 pounds
when captured . . . when liberated he was 82 pounds.
No food or water, frequent beatings, malaria, and they
were only occasionally let out of their cell to empty
their latrine bucket.

"Dana saw Ralph Lindley while they were outside
their cells one day, and the two men, 'who were best of
friends', didn't even recognize one another as they
stood there in their sunken, hollow bodies. After that
day, the two tapped out Morse code from their solitary
cells to communicate with one another and help keep
their sanity."

Dana—like Ralph—was in poor shape and nearly
lost his life in the Outram Road Prison. It was Marty
Govednik who convinced their liberators to transport

Dana to India immediately for medical care. Otherwise, he would have died.

In 1996 Betty Gillett and her persistent grandson, Chad Graves, finally received the Purple Heart medal Dana should have received fifty-one years earlier. The ceremony took place at U.S. Rep. Jim Kolbe's Tucson office. Chad was about eight years old when he realized his grandfather didn't have a Purple Heart. He knew his grandfather had suffered injuries in the crash of the *Postville Express*. He launched a mission to get that medal! He prompted Betty to right this wrong, and Marty Govednik helped by filing a report documenting Gillett's injuries. Six years later Chad's unending determination and Betty's work brought home M. Sgt. Harold "Dana" Gillett's Purple Heart. Chad was fourteen years old.

<u>Lt. Col. Donald J. Humphrey</u>

My next call was to Don Humphrey, pilot of the *Postville Express*. Patty, Don's wife, took my call. After a short time I asked, "Patty, is Don alive?" Patty said, "No, Don died February 17, 1999. He developed cancer, it got into the bone, and he died over the course of a year. It was pneumonia that finally took his life, but he died a peaceful death." Don was seventy-nine years old.

You'll recall "Hump" was from Postville, Iowa, but he settled in Kingston, Ohio, after the war. Patty's recap of the story went something like this: "Don and I dated a few times before he was shipped overseas. I didn't hear from him for two and a half years. I wrote him twice and sent him my graduation picture, but he never wrote back. Then one day in September 1945 my father calls me and says, 'You've got a telegram from Singapore from a Lt. Col. Humphrey. He wants to know if you're still interested.' At the time I was engaged to be married. My father asked me, 'What should I tell him?' I told my father to tell him, 'Yes, I'm interested!' There was something about this guy and I liked him. We were married in June 1946."

Patty and Don had two sons and two daughters. Today Patty lives just outside of Indianapolis in Fishers, Ind., near all four of her children.

<u>Lt. Col. Martin J. Govednik</u>

My final call was to Marty Govednik. LaVerne, his wife, gave me the news. Marty had died April 21, 1997 at the age of seventy-seven, after battling throat and lung cancer. Marty stayed in the military for twenty-four years and retired to a position in communications with General Dynamics, Ft. Worth, Tex. He retired again to become a math teacher for middle school children for nine more years.

LaVerne met Marty after the war. She said he talked about Outram Road Prison and the cruelty the Japanese subjected them to: their lack of even basic necessities such as food, water, hygiene, and clothing or bedding. Marty also fell victim to starvation. He went into prison weighing about 160 pounds . . . eight months later he was reduced to 85 pounds."

When I mentioned to LaVerne about the men being let out of their cells to empty their latrine buckets, LaVerne said, "There probably wasn't much in them, because they weren't getting food or water."

LaVerne spoke of a time when "the Japanese had Dana Gillett's head in a bucket of water and Govednik jumped the Japanese soldier to save his buddy. They let Gillett go and Govednik took a beating in his place." He would pass the time by etching out mathematics on his cell wall using a fish bone.

LaVerne told me Marty and my father were always involved in some antics together, like the time the two of them were stealing pies on their base in Kharagpur, India. LaVerne broke into laughter before finishing the story.

<u>Capt. Ernest "Cliff" Saltzman</u>

Saltz died possibly in 1972, though no one is quite certain when or how. Saltz never stayed in touch.

<u>T. Sgt. John A. MacDonald</u>

Mac dropped from sight nearly fifteen years ago. I'm told his health was bad. Betty Gillett is certain Mac died.

In the years that followed their homecoming, these men would gather for three or four days each year at reunions of the 468th Bomb Group and 20th Air Force. They would share stories, common experiences, and lasting friendships. Some found healing and the ability to fight the demons of war hiding behind their thoughts, dreams, and day-to-day living.

Today the crew of the *Postville Express* is together again, on the other side of tomorrow, and they live on.

"LET US NEVER FORGET. . ."